CENTENNIAL EDITION

NATIONAL PARKS GUIDE U.S.A.

Sarah Wassner Flynn
and Julie Beer

WASHINGTON, D.C.

Contents

Introduction:	
Our Amazing National Parks at 100!	6
How to Use This Book!	7
Map of National Parks in the United States	10

⇨ The East · 12
Introduction: The East	14
Acadia National Park	16
Everglades National Park	20
✪ A Man of Many Parks: Take a Teddy Tour!	24
Great Smoky Mountains National Park	26
Hot Springs National Park	30
✪ Explore America's Past in its National Parks	34
Other Must-see Park Properties	36

⇨ The Midwest · 38
Introduction: The Midwest	40
Badlands National Park	42
Cuyahoga Valley National Park	46
✪ Get Packing! Your National Park Suitcase Checklist	50
Theodore Roosevelt National Park	52
Wind Cave National Park	56
✪ The National Park Awesome Eight	60
Other Must-see Park Properties	62

⇨ The Southwest · 64
Introduction: The Southwest	66
Big Bend National Park	68
Carlsbad Caverns National Park	72
Grand Canyon National Park	76
✪ The National Parks' Other Dimension: Spooky Sites!	80
Other Must-see Park Properties	82

⇨ The West · 84
Introduction: The West	86
Bryce Canyon National Park	88
Denali National Park and Preserve	92
Glacier National Park	96
✪ Endangered Species Success Stories: Back From the Brink!	100
Grand Teton National Park	102
Haleakalā National Park	106
Hawai'i Volcanoes National Park	110
Joshua Tree National Park	114
Mount Rainier National Park	118
✪ Get the Scoop on Finding Fossils: Dig In!	122
Olympic National Park	124
Rocky Mountain National Park	128
Yellowstone National Park	132
Yosemite National Park	136

Hawai'i Volcanoes National Park, HI

Acadia National Park, ME

Carlsbad Caverns National Park, NM

Everglades National Park, FL

Zion National Park	140
⭐ By the Numbers! Record Setters in the National Parks	144
Other Must-see Park Properties	146

➔ More National Parks and Park Properties — 150

➔ 152-153
National Park of American Samoa
Arches National Park
Biscayne National Park
Black Canyon of the Gunnison National Park
Canyonlands National Park
Capitol Reef National Park

➔ 154-155
Channel Islands National Park
Congaree National Park
Dry Tortugas National Park
Gates of the Arctic National Park and Preserve
Glacier Bay National Park and Preserve
Great Basin National Park

➔ 156-157
Guadalupe Mountains National Park
Isle Royale National Park
Katmai National Park and Preserve
Kenai Fjords National Park
Kings Canyon National Park
Kobuk Valley National Park

➔ 158-159
Lake Clark National Park and Preserve
Lassen Volcanic National Park
Mammoth Cave National Park
Mesa Verde National Park
North Cascades National Park

➔ 160-161
Saguaro National Park
Sequoia National Park
Shenandoah National Park
Virgin Islands National Park
Voyageurs National Park

➔ 162
Wrangell-St. Elias National Park and Preserve

National Park Properties by State or Territory	163
Glossary/Find Out More	170
Index	172
Photo Credits	175

As you journey through the parks in this guide, see how many times you can spot Buddy Bison! Buddy is the mascot of the National Park Trust, an organization dedicated to inspiring kids to connect with nature and our amazing parklands. See page 176 for answer.

Our Amazing National Parks at 100!

In the last hundred years, life in the United States has changed a lot, but there are some places that remain unchanged, looking much as they did when the first European settlers arrived: the United States' national parks. These vast parcels of protected land, originally established as a way to protect the land and wildlife, contain more than 84 million acres (34 million ha) of stunning scenery and natural wonders—a true national treasure.

President Theodore Roosevelt is credited with championing the establishment of the parks. A concerned environmentalist, he made it his mission to ensure that these scenic spots would endure so that future generations could enjoy them. His dream has grown: Today in the United States, there are more than 400 protected properties, including national parks, monuments, battlefields, military parks, historical parks, historic sites, lakeshores, seashores, recreation areas, scenic rivers and trails, and the White House. Families flock to the parks for great American vacations that highlight both the nation's history and natural beauty. As part of the fun, kids can help learn more about the parks through the Junior Ranger Program, a series of hands-on activities designed to teach kids to explore and protect.

To celebrate the National Park Service's birthday, this Centennial Edition takes you on an adventure to many of these different and inspiring places through detailed entries and maps, as well as special feature spreads that highlight some of the best the parks have to offer—whether its history, adventure, or wildlife! You'll learn what to bring and how to get the most out of each park you visit!

AN AERIAL VIEW OF THE GRAND PRISMATIC SPRING IN YELLOWSTONE NATIONAL PARK, WYOMING

How to Use This Book!

Kids: Be sure to get parent or guardian permission before trying any of the activities mentioned in this book.

PARKS ARE INTRODUCED WITH FOUR PAGES OF INFORMATION, PHOTOS, AND A MAP.

③ RANGER TIPS WILL GIVE YOU IMPORTANT INFORMATION TO HELP YOU PREPARE FOR YOUR VISIT.

① THE NAME OF EACH PARK CAN BE FOUND IN THE "WELCOME TO" HEADING ON ITS OPENING PAGE.

④ FOR GREAT WAYS TO EXPLORE THE PARK, CHECK OUT THE ACTIVITIES ON THE "DISCOVER" PAGE.

⑤ THE COLORED TAB ON THE RIGHT SIDE OF THE PAGE HELPS TO IDENTIFY THE REGION YOU'RE IN.

② FOR BASIC FACTS ABOUT EACH PARK, CONSULT THE FACT BOX.

⑥ FOR EVEN MORE EXCITING THINGS TO ENJOY, BROWSE THE LIST OF THE FIVE MUST-DO ACTIVITIES IN EACH PARK.

⑦ FOR COOL AND EXCITING EXCURSIONS NEAR EACH NATIONAL PARK, CHECK OUT THE "DARE TO EXPLORE" SECTION.

⑧ FOR THE LOCATION OF VISITOR CENTERS AND OTHER PARK ATTRACTIONS, PERUSE THE PARK MAP. THE MINI LOCATOR MAP TELLS YOU WHAT STATE OR STATES THE PARK IS IN.

⑨ TO MAKE SURE YOU DON'T MISS ANYTHING FUN, KEEP TRACK OF YOUR ACTIVITIES WITH THE CHECKLIST FOUND HERE.

⑩ FOR A FUN AND UNIQUE BIT OF INFORMATION ABOUT EACH PARK, GO TO THE FUN FACT FOUND HERE.

7

① **THE TITLE OF THIS SECTION IS FOUND IN THE UPPER LEFT-HAND CORNER OF THE PAGE.**

② **THE NAMES OF PARK PROPERTIES APPEAR IN GREEN BOXES.**

OTHER MUST-SEE NATIONAL PARK PROPERTIES IN EACH REGION ARE INTRODUCED AT THE END OF THAT SECTION.

③ **FOR MORE INFORMATION ON ANY OF THE PARK PROPERTIES, GO TO THEIR WEBSITE. THE WEBSITE FOR EACH AREA CAN BE FOUND UNDER THE PROPERTY'S NAME.**

④ **THE LOCATION OF EACH PROPERTY IS FOUND NEXT TO ITS NAME. TO LOOK UP A STATE ABBREVIATION, LOOK ON THE LAST PAGE OF THE HOW TO USE SECTION.**

⑤ **FOR INFORMATION ABOUT WHAT MAKES EACH PROPERTY UNIQUE, CHECK OUT "WHY IT'S COOL." AND FOR GREAT IDEAS ON HOW TO SPEND YOUR TIME IN ANY OF THESE AREAS, LOOK FOR "WHAT TO DO" AND "TRY THIS."**

FOLLOWING THE FEATURED PARKS IS A SECTION ON SPOTLIGHTED PARKS— MORE INCREDIBLE DESTINATIONS TO ADD TO YOUR TRAVEL LIST.

⑥ **THE TITLE OF THIS SECTION IS FOUND IN THE UPPER LEFT-HAND CORNER OF THE PAGE.**

⑦ **THE NAMES OF ALL OF THE SPOTLIGHTED PARKS APPEAR IN GREEN BOXES.**

⑧ **LEARN BASIC FACTS ABOUT EACH SPOTLIGHTED PARK, GET RANGER TIPS, AND READ HIGHLIGHTS OF ACTIVITIES AND ANIMALS.**

8

NATIONAL PARK MAP KEY

- ① Bulleted feature
- ■ Point of interest
- • City
- ▲ Campground
- △ Elevation
- ↑N North arrow
- Overpass
- Dam
- Falls
- ○ Spring
- (77) U.S. Interstate highway
- (20) U.S. Federal highway
- (12) State highway
- (6) Provincial highway (Canadian)
- (22) Other road
- National boundary
- State boundary
- Continental Divide
- Road
- }====={ Tunnel
- ••••• Trail
- Railroad/Tram
- ••••• Ferry/Canoe route
- River
- Intermittent river
- National Park (N.P.) / National Park and Preserve / National Preserve / National Memorial Parkway
- National Grassland
- National Forest
- National Monument (Nat. Mon.) / National Wildlife Refuge
- Indian Reservation (U.S.) or Indian Reserve (Canadian)
- State Park
- Lake
- Glacier
- Swamp

LIST OF STATE AND TERRITORY ABBREVIATIONS

Alabama: AL
Alaska: AK
American Samoa: AS
Arizona: AZ
Arkansas: AR
California: CA
Colorado: CO
Connecticut: CT
Delaware: DE
District of Columbia: DC
Florida: FL
Georgia: GA
Guam: GU
Hawaii: HI

Idaho: ID
Illinois: IL
Indiana: IN
Iowa: IA
Kansas: KS
Kentucky: KY
Louisiana: LA
Maine: ME
Maryland: MD
Massachusetts: MA
Michigan: MI
Minnesota: MN
Mississippi: MS
Missouri: MO

Montana: MT
Nebraska: NE
Nevada: NV
New Hampshire: NH
New Jersey: NJ
New Mexico: NM
New York: NY
North Carolina: NC
North Dakota: ND
Ohio: OH
Oklahoma: OK
Oregon: OR
Pennsylvania: PA
Puerto Rico: PR

Rhode Island: RI
South Carolina: SC
South Dakota: SD
Tennessee: TN
Texas: TX
U.S. Virgin Islands: VI
Utah: UT
Vermont: VT
Virginia: VA
Washington: WA
West Virginia: WV
Wisconsin: WI
Wyoming: WY

the East

Everglades National Park

A Florida panther treks carefully through the wet and wild landscape of the Everglades, one of the East's most unique habitats.

the East

IN THE 1930s, increased automobile travel and new highways made the eastern region of the country more accessible than ever. As a result, people began flocking to this area and its national parks, which eventually became some of the most popular in the country. Today, the Northeast and Southeast remain magnets for national park enthusiasts. Three of this region's parks—Acadia, Great Smoky Mountains, and Shenandoah—receive millions of visitors each year.

Here, you'll pretty much see it all: thick forests, sparkling lakes, meandering streams, bubbling hot springs, and beaches rimmed by coral reefs. There are peaks towering nearly 7,000 feet (2,134 m) in the sky and deep caves carved out almost 400 feet (122 m) below the ground. There are parks set in the heart of the city, and others out in the wilderness. Rich historical sites highlight the birth and growth of our country. And wherever you roam, the diversity of the region's parks provides habitat for a wide variety of animals. Simply put, from the mountains meeting the sea in Acadia to the fields of flowers in Shenandoah, the region's biodiversity is breathtaking—and beyond vast.

Welcome to Acadia National Park!

Acadia may be one of the country's smallest national parks, but it's among the most popular places to visit, with more than two million people exploring this scenic spot in southern Maine each year. The park occupies two-thirds of Mount Desert Island as well as a collection of smaller islands and a portion of mainland Maine. In Acadia, you'll see glacial lakes, granite cliffs dropping into the ocean, sandy beaches, and dense forests. Hit some of the 120-plus miles (193-plus km) of hiking trails here and you'll be granted access to an up-close-and-personal tour of one of the most beautiful places in the world.

State: Maine
Established: February 26, 1919
Size: 47,748 acres (19,323 ha)
Website: nps.gov/acad

DISCOVER ACADIA

BEST VIEWS

Head to Schoodic Peninsula's six-mile (9.7-km) one-way loop, which offers great views of cool lighthouses, soaring seabirds, and forest-covered islands. It's also a great place to take a bike ride or go for a hike! Acadia Mountain (below) also offers stunning views of the park.

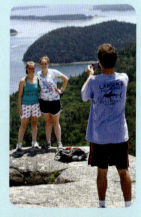

RANGER TIPS

Weather in Acadia changes often, so wear layers to be ready for any temperature. And if your trail goes along the ocean, make sure you know the tide schedule—during high tide, some pathways become covered in cold water.

TAKE IT EASY

Find a spot at Sand Beach, nestled along the rocky shores of Mount Desert Island (top). Fly a kite with the help of the cool breeze blowing off the ocean, sink your feet into the crushed-shell sand, or brave a splash in the 55°F (13°C) surf. For warmer waters, head to Echo Lake Beach.

BE EXTREME

Want to scale new heights? Climbers of all ages and abilities can take rock-climbing classes (center) with companies like Acadia Mountain Guides, and "learn the ropes" of scaling Acadia's pink-granite cliffs.

ALL ABOUT ANIMALS

Stand along the shore of Mount Desert Island and you'll likely see one of the 270 species of birds that call Acadia home, including bald eagles and peregrine falcons. You may also spot harbor seals, white-tailed deer (below), red foxes, beavers, black bears, and even a breaching humpback whale out in the ocean.

Oh, My Mountain

1 Check out Cadillac Mountain (below), which, at 1,530 feet (466 m) tall, is the tallest peak on the Atlantic coast north of Brazil. Drive to the top, then take in unrivaled panoramic views while following a 0.3-mile (0.5-km) trail around the summit.

Ride On

2 Grab a bike and pedal along the park's 45 miles (72.4 km) of scenic carriage roads, which wind throughout the park and are closed off to cars. You can also opt to travel some of the roads by a horse-drawn carriage, starting from Wildwood Stables.

Light It Up

3 Explore the grounds surrounding the Bass Harbor Lighthouse (left) on Mount Desert Island. Built in 1858, the lighthouse is still fully functional, warning approaching boats of the Bass Harbor Bar, a large sandbar connecting downtown Bar Harbor to Bar Island.

Cruise By

4 From mid-May to October, take the ranger-led Islesford Historical Cruise. You'll make a 45-minute stop at Little Cranberry Island's Islesford Historical Museum for a trip back in time to the tiny island's maritime past.

Into the Wild

5 The Sieur de Monts is the site of the Nature Center and the Abbe Museum (left), where you can learn about the culture and traditions of Maine Native Americans. It's also the site of the Wild Gardens of Acadia and the start of many hikes throughout the park.

[DARE TO EXPLORE]

ALL ABOUT THE OCEAN
Get hands-on with the aquatic animals of the area at the Mount Desert Oceanarium in Bar Harbor, one of the few remaining lobster hatcheries in the world. **theoceanarium.com**

HOLE IN ONE
For some post-park fun, hit Pirate's Cove Miniature Golf in Bar Harbor, where you can putt around an authentic, full-size pirate ship, under waterfalls, and through caves. **piratescove.net**

WHALE-WATCH
During the summer, head out on the ocean on a whale-watching boat. Keep your eyes peeled for a playful humpback, which just may leap out of the water right in front of you! **barharborwhales.com**

PICK BLUEBERRIES
From mid-July through August, blueberries are bountiful throughout Maine, including the sunnier spots in Acadia National Park. Grab a bucket and hit the trails leading up to Champlain or Cadillac Mountains, where you're sure to snag a sweet snack.

MY CHECKLIST

- ✓ Listen to waves crashing on the shore at Thunder Hole Rock Cavern.
- ✓ Drive the Park Loop.
- ✓ Bike, hike, or take a horse-drawn carriage tour along carriage roads.
- ✓ Learn about the park's plants and wildlife at an exhibit at the Nature Center.
- ✓ Stroll the Schoodic Peninsula.
- ✓ Look for creatures, like crabs and sea stars, in tide pools along the coast.
- ✓ Hop on a ranger-narrated boat cruise.

FAST FACT: The light in the Bass Harbor Lighthouse has been used continuously for more than 150 years.

19

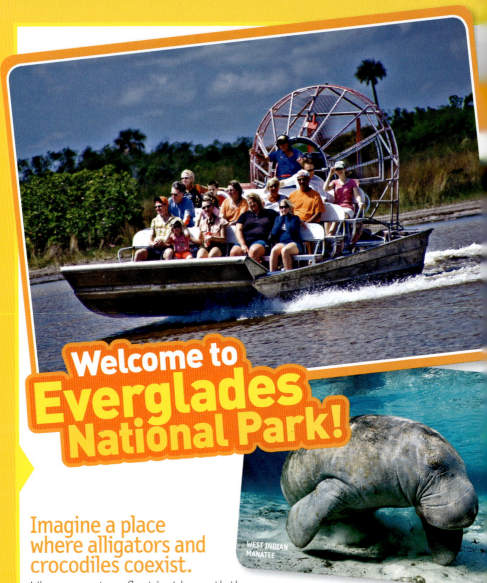

WEST INDIAN MANATEE

Welcome to Everglades National Park!

Imagine a place where alligators and crocodiles coexist.

Where manatees float just beneath the surface of a slow-moving river. And where panthers prowl the dense tropical woodlands. That's just what you'll find in Everglades National Park, a protected area of wetlands in southeast Florida. Made up of marshes, swamps, a river, and a bay, Everglades serves as host to an abundance of wildlife, from algae to alligators. It's here where more than 1,000 kinds of plants, 120 types of trees, and countless animals (including many on the endangered species list) grow and thrive, making Everglades one of the most ecologically diverse parks on the planet.

State: Florida
Established: December 6, 1947
Size: 1,542,526 acres (624,239 ha)
Website: nps.gov/ever

DISCOVER EVERGLADES

RANGER TIPS

Wear long pants, cover your arms, and spray on insect repellent to avoid mosquitoes, which are around all year long. Also leave the wildlife alone (below) and avoid collecting plants, an activity prohibited in the park.

TAKE IT EASY

Unwind and eat at designated picnic spots, including Paurotis Pond, Nine Mile Pond, and West Lake. You can also take a half-mile (0.8-km) walk around Flamingo Bay, a protected marine nursery.

BE EXTREME

Kayak out to the park's Ten Thousand Islands (below). You'll get unrivaled views from the water while cutting through mangroves and oyster beds. Don't be surprised if you're suddenly surrounded by feeding manatees or friendly dolphins!

BEST VIEWS

Take a bike ride along Tram Road and stop at the halfway point, where you'll find a 65-foot (19.8-m)-high observation tower (above). Climb to the top and be rewarded with an unobstructed panoramic view of the Everglades.

ALL ABOUT ANIMALS

Home to a host of wildlife, the Everglades is a unique place, where you'll see dozens of endangered species in their natural habitat, including the swallowtail butterfly, leatherback turtle (below), West Indian manatee, and Florida panther.

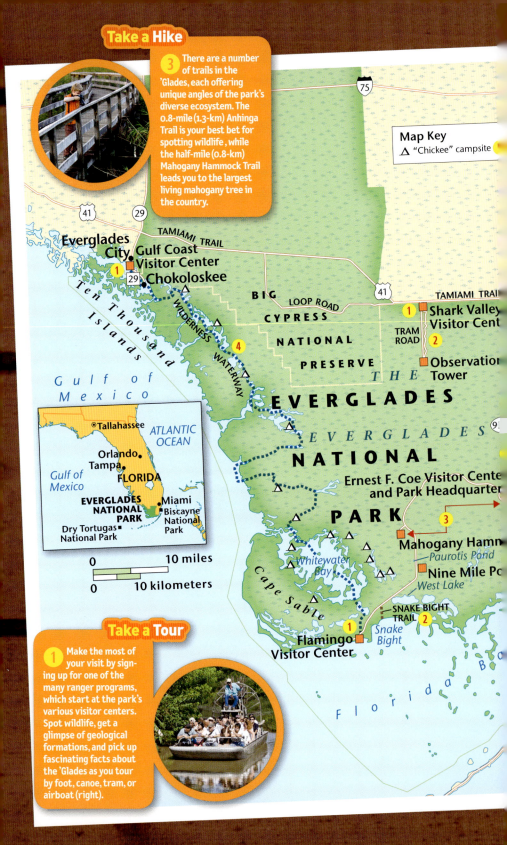

Go Fish

4 Hop in a canoe or kayak and cast a line into the inland and coastal waters of the Everglades and see if you can reel in fish like snapper, sea trout, bass, and bluegill. A fishing license is required within the park; check in with the visitor center for information about fishing tours and boat rentals.

Set Up Camp

5 From the beach to the woods, you can camp out throughout the park. Check out the "chickees"—elevated camping platforms—(left) available in various spots. Permits are required, so call the visitor center before your trip. (Note: None of these chickees are available by car.)

Ride On

2 Bike the 15-mile (24.1-km) scenic loop at Shark Valley (left), an excellent way to view the 'Glades at your own pace. The trip takes two to three hours and there are no shortcuts, so make sure you're up to the task. For a less strenuous ride, bike along the Snake Bight Trail, one of the park's best bird-watching trails. Don't let the name deter you! In this play on words, a "bight" is actually a bay (Snake Bight) within a larger bay (Florida Bay).

[DARE TO EXPLORE]

PARK HOP
There are other equally amazing parks and preserves within a quick drive from Everglades. Take day trips to Biscayne National Park (20 miles [32.2 km] east, home of the northernmost living coral reef in the continental United States and great for snorkeling and glass-bottom boat rides); Dry Tortugas National Park (check out an abandoned 19th-century brick fortress and more than 250 shipwrecks); or Big Cypress National Preserve (the H. P. Williams and Oasis Wildlife Viewing Platforms are excellent for alligator scoping).

BIG BOUNTY
Stroll the grounds of the Fruit & Spice Park in nearby Homestead, Florida, where more than 500 varieties of fruits (including 75 types of bananas alone!), vegetables, and nuts grow. Hungry? Munch on some of the park's samplings at the Mango Café.
fruitandspicepark.org

STONE HOME
Check out Coral Castle—just north of Homestead—a sculpture carved out of more than 1,100 tons (998 MT) of coral rock that took one man almost 30 years to build! Take a tour to learn how he did it and to see cool features, like functioning rocking chairs, a telescope, and a 9-ton (8.2-MT) gate that moves with just the touch of a finger—all made entirely out of stone.
coralcastle.com

MY CHECKLIST
- ✓ Meet up with a park ranger for a fun guided tour by foot or by boat.
- ✓ Pedal around Shark Valley or the Snake Bight Trail.
- ✓ Paddle in a canoe or kayak to enjoy views on the water.
- ✓ Hike the 150-plus miles (241-plus km) of nature trails the park has to offer.
- ✓ Take a two-hour, narrated tour of the Tamiami Trail on an open-air tram.
- ✓ Check out the oldest living mahogany tree in the U.S.
- ✓ Enjoy a picnic at Paurotis Pond, Nine Mile Pond, or West Lake.

FAST FACT: The Everglades are home to more than 200,000 alligators and crocodiles.

CENTENNIAL EDITION

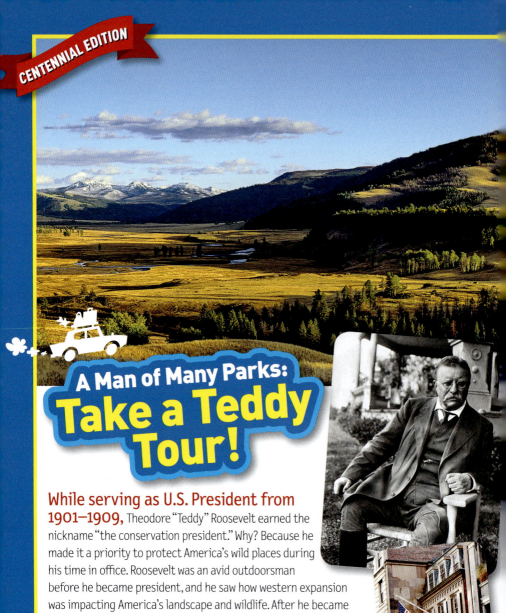

A Man of Many Parks:
Take a Teddy Tour!

While serving as U.S. President from 1901–1909, Theodore "Teddy" Roosevelt earned the nickname "the conservation president." Why? Because he made it a priority to protect America's wild places during his time in office. Roosevelt was an avid outdoorsman before he became president, and he saw how western expansion was impacting America's landscape and wildlife. After he became president, he doubled the amount of sites in the parks system to preserve these wild places. By the time he left office, Roosevelt had established five national parks and proclaimed 18 national monuments—protecting more than 230 million acres (93 million ha) of land!

Besides being represented on South Dakota's Mount Rushmore National Memorial (see page 63), Theodore Roosevelt is honored with a national park in his name in North Dakota (see page 52). Here are some other stops on the Teddy Tour!

> Roosevelt was a boxer. One day, while sparring in the White House, he took a punch that left him nearly **BLIND IN ONE EYE.**

TOP: Yellowstone National Park
CENTER: Theodore Roosevelt
BOTTOM: Roosevelt's birthplace in New York City

24

STOP ONE
THEODORE ROOSEVELT BIRTHPLACE NATIONAL HISTORIC SITE

Theodore Roosevelt was the only president born in New York City, and his birthplace is now a national historic site. In the house, you will find several teddy bears, which were named after the president when he refused to shoot a bear cub. Check out the bullet-pierced eyeglass case that helped save his life during an assassination attempt. Also in New York, on Long Island, is Sagamore Hill—Roosevelt's "summer White House," which was his home for more than 30 years until his death in 1919. The 23-room national historic site is furnished just the way it was during his presidency.

STOP TWO
CRATER LAKE NATIONAL PARK

The waters of Oregon's Crater Lake National Park, the first of five national parks Roosevelt established, are so dark they look like ink. The lake is in a dormant volcano that erupted in 5700 B.C. The eruption was so massive that the summit of the volcano collapsed, creating a caldera, which, over time, filled with rain and snowmelt, resulting in Crater Lake. The lake is 1,943 feet (592 m) deep, making it the deepest lake in the U.S.

STOP THREE
THEODORE ROOSEVELT ISLAND

How fitting that the president who embraced nature has a memorial in Washington, D.C., that is all about the outdoors. Theodore Roosevelt Island sits in the Potomac River, a stone's throw from the city. The island's Swamp Trail is a 1.5-mile (2.4-km) loop that passes through swampy woods and a cattail marsh. Visit the bronze statue of Teddy (below) to see how he looked giving one of his famous speeches.

After negotiating peace in the Russo-Japanese war, Roosevelt became the **FIRST AMERICAN** to win the Nobel Peace Prize.

STOP FOUR
YOSEMITE NATIONAL PARK

While Roosevelt was in office, he spent three nights camping in California's Yosemite National Park (above) with famed naturalist John Muir. During the trip, they slept under the stars and visited now-famous vistas, and Muir convinced Roosevelt to include Yosemite Valley as part of the larger Yosemite National Park.

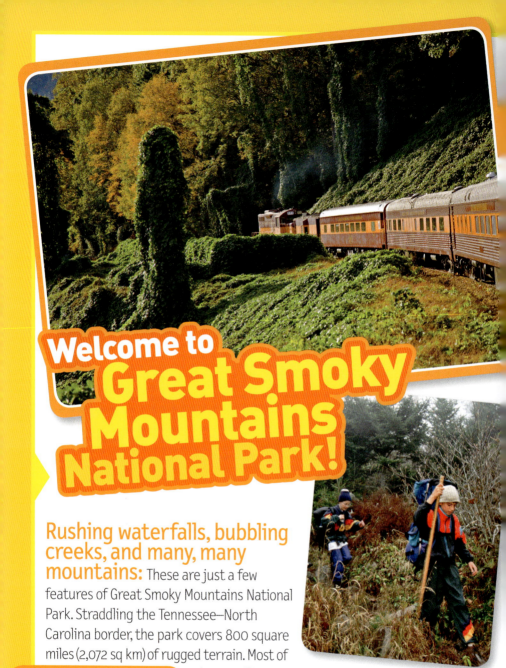

Welcome to Great Smoky Mountains National Park!

Rushing waterfalls, bubbling creeks, and many, many mountains: These are just a few features of Great Smoky Mountains National Park. Straddling the Tennessee–North Carolina border, the park covers 800 square miles (2,072 sq km) of rugged terrain. Most of the 10 million yearly visitors see the sights by car, taking a drive on the 384 miles (779 km) of mountain roads running through the park. But there's plenty to see by foot, too, thanks to the seemingly unending hiking trails that take you through the Smokies' dense forests and up the craggy peaks.

States: North Carolina and Tennessee
Established: June 15, 1934
Size: 521,085 acres (210,876 ha)
Website: nps.gov/grsm

DISCOVER
GREAT SMOKY MOUNTAINS

RANGER TIPS

Want to spot wildlife? Head out in the morning or evening to open areas like Cataloochee or Cades Cove.

TAKE IT EASY

Pack a picnic and seek out a shady spot at one of the many picnic areas in the park. Chimneys, a wooded area on the Tennessee side of the Smokies, has tables overlooking the West Prong of the Little Pigeon River. Or take a stroll on the many quiet trails (top).

BE EXTREME

Soar to new heights by hiking the trail to Ramsey Cascades (below), the tallest waterfall in the park. Just make sure you've got the climb in you: Eight miles (12.9 km) round trip and escalating 2,000 feet (610 m) in elevation, it's considered a very challenging hike.

BEST VIEWS

From April to November, head up to the observation platform (left) on top of Clingmans Dome. There's no higher point in the park—and no better view of the Smokies. (Note: Air pollution is an issue: On clear days views expand over 100 miles [161 km]. Unfortunately, air pollution often limits viewing distances to under 20 miles [32.2 km].)

ALL ABOUT ANIMALS

There's a reason the American black bear (below) is the symbol of the Smokies: Roughly 1,500 of them live here (that's two bears per square mile [2.6 sq km])! This protected habitat is also home to deer, elk, and a whopping 30 species of salamanders. Of the 240 species of birds found in the park, 60 are year-round residents.

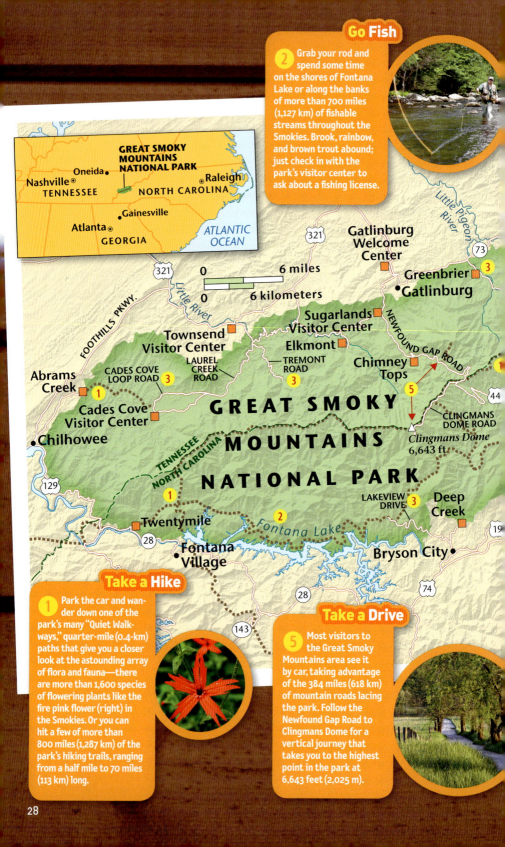

Go Fish

2 Grab your rod and spend some time on the shores of Fontana Lake or along the banks of more than 700 miles (1,127 km) of fishable streams throughout the Smokies. Brook, rainbow, and brown trout abound; just check in with the park's visitor center to ask about a fishing license.

Take a Hike

1 Park the car and wander down one of the park's many "Quiet Walkways," quarter-mile (0.4-km) paths that give you a closer look at the astounding array of flora and fauna—there are more than 1,600 species of flowering plants like the fire pink flower (right) in the Smokies. Or you can hit a few of more than 800 miles (1,287 km) of the park's hiking trails, ranging from a half mile to 70 miles (113 km) long.

Take a Drive

5 Most visitors to the Great Smoky Mountains area see it by car, taking advantage of the 384 miles (618 km) of mountain roads lacing the park. Follow the Newfound Gap Road to Clingmans Dome for a vertical journey that takes you to the highest point in the park at 6,643 feet (2,025 m).

Pedal On

3 Although many park roads are too dangerous—or too steep—for bikes, some, like the 11-mile (17.7-km) Cades Cove Loop, are very popular with cyclists. Other areas, such as Greenbrier, Lakeview Drive, Tremont Road, and Cataloochee Valley, are also great places to ride.

Go Back in Time

4 Stop by the Mountain Farm Museum, adjacent to the Oconaluftee Visitor Center. Learn what life was like there hundreds of years ago by exploring centuries-old farm buildings (right) and watching demonstrations by park employees, like how the pioneers produced their own cornmeal and flour.

[DARE TO EXPLORE]

PARK IT
About 100 miles (161 km) northwest of the Great Smoky Mountains, straddling Tennessee and Kentucky, is the Big South Fork National River and Recreation Area. Hike, horseback ride, fish, swim, camp, and gawk at waterfalls sure to wow you. **nps.gov/biso**

FOREST FUN
Want more wilderness? Chattahoochee-Oconee National Forest in Gainesville, Georgia (about 95 miles [153 km] from Great Smoky Mountains), is home to a mix of lakes, streams, valleys, and Brasstown Bald, Georgia's highest mountain at 4,784 feet (1,458 m). Enter the forest's name in the search bar at **fs.fed.us**.

WET AND WILD
There are no actual wild bears here—but plenty of wild rides! At the Wild Bear Falls Water Park in Gatlinburg, Tennessee (about 3 miles [4.8 km] from Great Smoky Mountains), you can float in an inner tube down a lazy river, zoom down slippery slides, and be doused by a huge bucket spilling 300 gallons (1,136 L) of water from above! **wgwildbearfalls.com**

ALL ABOARD
Climb on the Great Smoky Mountains Railroad in Bryson City, North Carolina. Watch with awe as Western North Carolina—and its lush green valleys and river gorges—passes by as you chug along. **gsmr.com**

MY CHECKLIST

✓ Hit the hiking trails and check out a waterfall or beautiful trees, plants, and flowers.

✓ Visit the Mountain Farm Museum to learn about life in the Smokies 100 years ago.

✓ Climb to the top of the observation tower on Clingmans Dome.

✓ Go on a bike ride around Cades Cove Loop.

✓ See the Smokies by car on hundreds of miles of mountain roads.

✓ Look for mammals and birds within the Smokies' deciduous forests.

✓ Seek out salamanders in a stream.

FAST FACT: There are more than 2,000 miles (3,219 km) of streams in the Smokies.

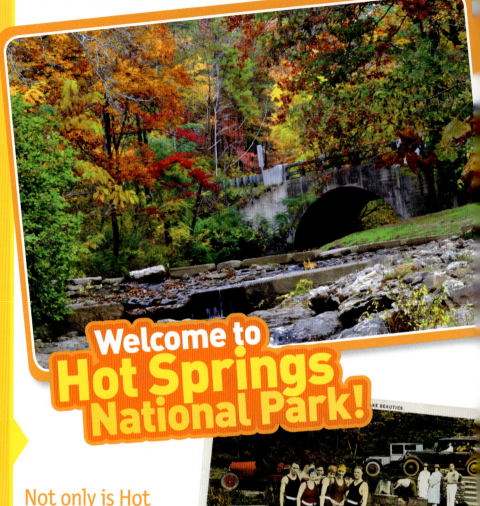

Welcome to Hot Springs National Park!

Not only is Hot Springs one of the country's oldest national parks— it's also the smallest. But what Hot Springs lacks in size it makes up for in character: Set against the backdrop of a mostly urban area, the park is distinguished by its 47 mineral springs, from which a million gallons (3.8 million L) of thermal (143°F [62°C]) water spout each day. Whether visitors sip the water or bathe in it, the park's famous hot springs fascinate people from around the world as much today as they did decades ago.

State: Arkansas
Established: March 4, 1921
Size: 5,500 acres (2,226 ha)
Website: nps.gov/hosp

DISCOVER HOT SPRINGS

RANGER TIPS

Drink the water. Tested regularly, the spring water spouting from designated drinking fountains is odorless, fresh tasting, and safe to sip.

TAKE IT EASY

Dip your toes in the thermal waters as you relax and enjoy the lushness of Arlington Lawn Park in downtown Hot Springs. For a relaxing walk, stroll along the Grand Promenade, a half-mile (0.8-km), landscaped brick walkway that begins behind the Fordyce Bathhouse Visitor Center (below).

BE EXTREME

Visit the Hot Springs pool in Arlington Rock, where you can see and touch the water. Be careful, it's hot! Every year about 700,000 gallons (2.6 million L) of 143°F (62°C) water flow from the springs.

BEST VIEWS

The Hot Springs Mountain observation tower (below) elevates you 1,256 feet (383 m) above sea level. On a clear day, you can see views extending up to 40 miles (64.4 km) on all sides.

ALL ABOUT ANIMALS

Hot Springs National Park is all about amphibians, including toads, salamanders, and frogs. Reptiles, like the anole lizard (below), live here, too. A bevy of birds also call Hot Springs home; keep your eyes peeled for herons, owls, roadrunners, and woodpeckers.

HOT SPRINGS NATIONAL PARK — ARKANSAS
- Ouachita National Forest
- Little Rock
- Magic Springs & Crystal Falls
- Crater of Diamonds State Park

Fill Up

2 Take an empty jug to the Thermal Water Jug Fountain on Bathhouse Row and fill it up with fresh-tasting mineral water from the hot springs. Want a cool drink? Take your jug to the Happy Hollow or Whittington cold-water springs.

Tour the Baths

1 Find out why Hot Springs was once known as the "American Spa" by touring Bathhouse Row, the site of eight bathhouses built in the early 20th century. Start at the Fordyce Bathhouse (left), which serves as the park's visitor center.

Map labels

- HOT SPRINGS NATIONAL PARK
- SUGARLOAF MOUNTAIN
- CITY OF HOT SPRINGS
- Hot Springs Creek
- HOT SPRINGS NATIONAL PARK
- PARK AVENUE
- Happy Hollow Spring
- **3** HOT SPRINGS MOUNTAIN DRIVE
- Hot Springs Mt. Tower 1,040 ft
- WHITTINGTON AVENUE
- 7
- FOUNTAIN ST.
- Arlington Lawn
- **4** PEAK TRAIL
- GRAND PROMENADE
- HOT SPRINGS MOUNTAIN
- Whittington Spring
- DRIVE
- Bathhouse Row
- **1** Fordyce Bathhouse (Visitor Center)
- WEST MOUNTAIN
- WEST MOUNTAIN SUMMIT DRIVE
- Thermal Water Jug Fountain
- City Visitor Center
- HOT SPRINGS NATIONAL PARK
- 1,100 ft
- PROSPECT AVENUE
- CITY OF HOT SPRINGS
- CENTRAL AVENUE
- Hot Springs Creek
- MALVERN AVENUE
- GRAND AVE
- 70B
- 70B 270B
- 270B

Take a Drive

3 Drive up the winding and scenic Hot Springs and North Mountain Roads to the top of Hot Springs Mountain, where you can catch stunning views from an observation tower.

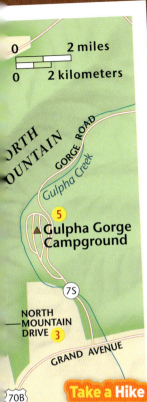

[DARE TO EXPLORE]

FOLLOW THE FOREST
Explore the nearby Ouachita National Forest, the oldest national forest in the South. About 10 miles (16.1 km) west of Hot Springs, you can connect with a mountain road that will lead you to hidden nooks and spectacular views.
www.fs.usda.gov/ouachita

MAGIC RIDE
Take a dip—and do a flip!—at Magic Springs & Crystal Falls, the only theme park within a national park. Zoom down a water slide, spin around on a carousel, or zip around on lightning-quick roller coasters and rides. **magicsprings.com**

DIAMOND HUNT
Look for a diamond in the rough at Crater of Diamonds State Park in Murfreesboro (about 60 miles [96.6 km] from Hot Springs). Scour a plowed field and try to spy diamonds in every color of the rainbow, plus plenty of other precious stones, rocks, and minerals.
craterofdiamondsstatepark.com

SECRET GARDEN
Take a relaxed nature walk through Garvan Woodland botanical gardens, a 210-acre (85-ha) park nestled alongside picturesque Lake Hamilton in Hot Springs. In the spring, follow trails that burst with blooms and trees in every type and color.
garvangardens.com

Take a Hike

4 Between the bathhouses and the mountains are 27 miles (43.5 km) of wooded trails. Want a challenge? Tackle the Peak, a half-mile (0.8-km) climb that leads to the summit of Hot Springs Mountain (access it from the Grand Promenade).

Camp Out

5 Pitch a tent and sleep under the stars at Gulpha Gorge Campground (right) next to rushing rapids or a babbling brook.

MY CHECKLIST
- ✓ Take a tour of the historic bath houses on Bathhouse Row.
- ✓ Stroll down the Grand Promenade.
- ✓ Camp out or play at Gulpha Gorge Campground.
- ✓ Get whisked to the top of the Hot Springs Mountain observation tower.
- ✓ Fill up a jug of hot or cold water straight from the springs.
- ✓ Look for frogs and other critters in Gulpha Gorge Creek.
- ✓ Relax in the shade in Arlington Lawn Park.

FAST FACT: Water from the hot springs fell as rain when the pyramids of Egypt were built—4,400 years ago!

CENTENNIAL EDITION

EXPLORE AMERICA'S PAST IN ITS
NATIONAL PARKS

Some national parks celebrate America's unique and pristine landscapes, while others memorialize events from our country's past through monuments and buildings that serve as reminders. When you visit these national parks and monuments you can explore America's history.

BOSTON NATIONAL HISTORICAL PARK

THE PLACE: Massachusetts

THE HISTORY: Called the "Cradle of Liberty," Boston's historic monuments and sites collectively tell the story of American independence and the Revolutionary War. Boston National Historical Park is a 43-acre (17-ha) park that includes parts of downtown Boston, Charlestown, and South Boston.

WHAT TO SEE:

★ USS *Constitution*—The world's oldest commissioned warship still afloat sits in the Charlestown Navy Yard. First launched in 1797, it defeated four British frigates and earned the nickname "Old Ironsides" in the War of 1812.

★ Paul Revere House—It is now a museum honoring the famous silversmith who alerted the colonial militia of incoming British forces. Paul Revere and his family lived here between 1770 and 1800.

★ Bunker Hill National Monument—A 20-story obelisk (right) marks this first major battle of the American Revolution, fought on June 17, 1775.

STATUE OF LIBERTY & ELLIS ISLAND

THE PLACE: New Jersey / New York

THE HISTORY: In 1886, the Statue of Liberty, a gift from France to the United States, was dedicated on Liberty Island in New York Harbor. Nearby is Ellis Island, where 12 million immigrants checked in on their way to the United States between 1892 and 1924.

WHAT TO SEE:

★ Lady Liberty—You can take a ferry to Liberty Island and just visit the grounds and gaze up at the 305-foot (93-m) statue. Or, you can reserve ahead and get a ticket to go inside the pedestal and museum. A separate reservation also gets you to the statue's crown.

★ Your family's name—Just like the immigrants arriving long ago, visitors arrive at Ellis Island (above) by boat. Search for names of your ancestors on the immigrant wall of honor. Tours—including audio tours for kids—describe the history of the island.

LITTLE BIGHORN BATTLEFIELD NATIONAL MONUMENT

LOCATION: Montana

THE HISTORY: Visitors to the Little Bighorn Battlefield National Monument can get a deeper understanding of that two-day battle, which took place June 25–26, 1876, in Montana Territory between the U.S. Army's 7th Calvary and the Lakota, Sioux, Arapaho, and Cheyenne who fought them. Located on the Crow Indian Reservation, the monument includes a visitor center, museum, Custer National Cemetery (below), and Last Stand memorial.

THINGS TO DO:

★ Tour the battlefield—In all, 263 soldiers, including the controversial Lt. Col. George Armstrong Custer, died in the battle, along with about 100 Lakota, Arapaho, and Cheyenne who were defending their way of life.

★ Visit the cemetery—In 1881, white marble markers accounting for all the U.S. soldiers who fell were erected at the site. In 1999, markers were erected on the sites where Native American warriors were known to have died.

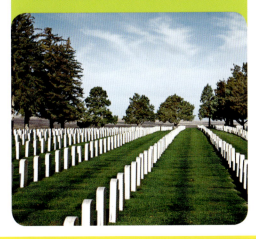

NATIONAL MALL & MEMORIAL PARKS

THE PLACE: Washington, D.C.

THE HISTORY: The National Mall stretches two miles (3.2 km) long and is spread over 1,000 acres (405 ha) of green space in the middle of the capital city. Major Pierre Charles L'Enfant was selected by President George Washington to design the nation's capital. He envisioned it as a grand city built around open space, which became the National Mall.

WHAT TO SEE:

★ National Mall monuments—All are open 24 hours a day and are free to the public. The Mall is pedestrian-friendly, but you can also bike, Segway, or take a hop-on/hop-off bus to see all the sites.

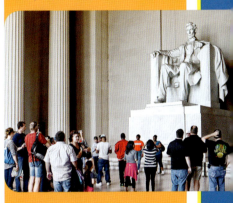

★ The Lincoln Memorial—You know this memorial from the "tails" side of a penny! Inside the marble building is a 19-foot (5.8-m)-tall statue of President Lincoln (above).

★ Dr. Martin Luther King, Jr., Memorial—Although not a president, civil rights leader Martin Luther King, Jr., made his mark on the country. The statue (below), located near the Lincoln Memorial, pays tribute to King's stands on freedom, liberty, and justice.

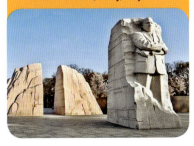

⮕ Other Must-see Park Properties in the East

ASSATEAGUE ISLAND NATIONAL SEASHORE (MD, VA)

nps.gov/asis

WHY IT'S COOL: Wild ponies roam this park's sandy beaches.

WHAT TO DO: Watch for wildlife as you cruise the coastline; swimming, camping, boating, and fishing.

TRY THIS: Explore the island by bike as you peddle through the different coastal habitats.

CAPE COD NATIONAL SEASHORE (MA)

nps.gov/caco

WHY IT'S COOL: It's an "arm" of sandy beaches, wetlands, salt marshes, and woodlands.

WHAT TO DO: Explore historic lighthouses; hiking, biking, swimming, and surfing.

TRY THIS: Watch films about Cape Cod at the Salt Pond Visitor Center.

CAPTAIN JOHN SMITH CHESAPEAKE NATIONAL HISTORIC TRAIL (VA, MD, DE, DC, PA, NY)

nps.gov/cajo

WHY IT'S COOL: It follows John Smith's travels in the Chesapeake Bay and the rivers that flow into it.

WHAT TO DO: Visit Historic Jamestowne Island; sailing, kayaking, hiking, boating, swimming, and bird-watching.

TRY THIS: Explore an Indian village at the Jefferson Patterson Park and Museum in St. Leonard, Maryland.

COLONIAL NATIONAL HISTORICAL PARK (VA)

nps.gov/colo

WHY IT'S COOL: It protects the sites of Historic Jamestowne and Yorktown Battlefield.

WHAT TO DO: Tour the park's historic areas and walk or bike the Battlefield Tour roads.

TRY THIS: Join the Pinch Pot Program to learn how Native Americans and English settlers made and used pottery.

DELAWARE WATER GAP NATIONAL RECREATION AREA (NJ, PA)

nps.gov/dewa

WHY IT'S COOL: It is home to the Middle Delaware River, one of the cleanest rivers in the U.S., plus plenty of wildlife, waterfalls, and trails.

WHAT TO DO: Swimming, fishing, boating, canoeing, kayaking, rafting, and tubing.

TRY THIS: Check out the world-famous "Water Gap," where the Delaware River cuts through the Appalachian Mountains.

FORT SUMTER NATIONAL MONUMENT (SC)

nps.gov/fosu

WHY IT'S COOL: It's the spot that sparked the American Civil War.

WHAT TO DO: Tour historic forts; boating, fishing, kayaking, and bird-watching.

TRY THIS: Check out the Fort Sumter museum to learn how the fort was built.

GULF ISLANDS NATIONAL SEASHORE (FL, MS)

nps.gov/guis

WHY IT'S COOL: This scenic spot offers white sandy beaches, blue water, and glimpses of forts that date back almost 150 years.

WHAT TO DO: Check out historic forts; swimming, snorkeling, fishing, hiking, boating, biking, and strolling along the beach.

TRY THIS: Camp out at Fort Pickens and set out on some of the surrounding scenic hiking trails.

HARRIET TUBMAN UNDERGROUND RAILROAD NATIONAL MONUMENT (MD)

nps.gov/hatu

WHY IT'S COOL: It honors the Underground Railroad's most well-known conductor, who led 70 enslaved people to freedom.

WHAT TO DO: Learn about the heroine at the Harriet Tubman Museum, and visit important sites from her early life in Maryland.

TRY THIS: Visit the Jacob Jackson Home Site, once owned by a free African American man who secretly helped Tubman communicate with her family.

KENNESAW MOUNTAIN NATIONAL BATTLEFIELD PARK (GA)

nps.gov/kemo

WHY IT'S COOL: This is where some of the heaviest fighting of the Civil War's Atlanta campaign took place.

WHAT TO DO: Visit battlefields and see monuments to the soldiers who fought here.

TRY THIS: Hike 1.2 miles (1.9 km) to the top of Kennesaw Mountain, 1,808 feet (551 m) above sea level.

PATERSON GREAT FALLS NATIONAL HISTORICAL PARK (NJ)

nps.gov/pagr

WHY IT'S COOL: It's the site of one of America's first industrial cities.

WHAT TO DO: Check out the spectacular waterfalls.

TRY THIS: Join the park rangers for a free one-hour outdoor tour.

SALEM MARITIME NATIONAL HISTORIC SITE (MA)

nps.gov/sama

WHY IT'S COOL: It's one of the most important ports in the United States.

WHAT TO DO: Tour Salem Maritime's historic buildings and walk around the city of Salem.

TRY THIS: Visit the *Friendship*, a reconstruction of a 171-foot (52.1-m)-tall three-masted ship built in 1797.

WRIGHT BROTHERS NATIONAL MEMORIAL (NC)

nps.gov/wrbr

WHY IT'S COOL: It's the site of the first powered flight.

WHAT TO DO: Visit the spot where the Wright brothers first took off and landed; tour the park's museums and exhibits.

TRY THIS: Participate in programs like "Kite Flight," in which you see how a kite is made and test one out.

the Midwest

Theodore Roosevelt National Park

A herd of beautiful wild horses runs across the wide-open spaces of Theodore Roosevelt National Park in North Dakota.

the Midwest

NESTLED IN BETWEEN the Appalachians and the Rocky Mountains, the Midwest parks offer a variety pack of landscapes, from the grand Great Lakes to the sweeping sandstone cliffs of the badlands. Mile upon mile of prairies and cornfields make up most of the Midwest, and the area's national parks let you roam free among these seemingly endless grasslands. The spirit of America's frontier is preserved in the rugged scenery and untouched acres that are showcased in the Midwest national parks.

That's not to say the Midwest is all fields and flowers—it is also home to urban national parks, including Jefferson National Expansion Memorial in St. Louis (where you'll find the Gateway Arch) and Cuyahoga Valley near Cleveland, Ohio (visit waterfalls galore!). These areas are incredibly rich in history—one park, for example, traces the route taken by the Lewis and Clark expedition to the Pacific Ocean in the early 1800s, and another is named in honor of President Theodore Roosevelt, who became enchanted with this unique area back in 1883.

And if that's not enough, there are ancient rock formations to gawk at and a massive network of underground passages to explore. Not to mention there's plenty of wildlife, too: Deer, pronghorn, bison, reptiles, and of course the prairie dog can all be spotted during your visit to the Midwest.

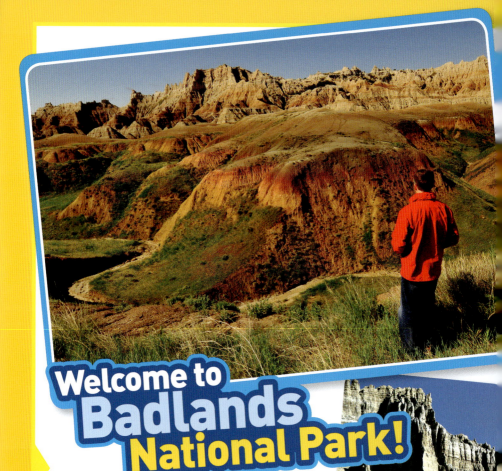

Welcome to Badlands National Park!

Early French-Canadian trappers

named it *les mauvaises terres à traverser.* Translation? "Bad lands to cross." But there's nothing bad to say about this extremely unique region. Famous for its towering, jagged cliffs, steep-walled canyons, and bumpy gray terrain, the rocky landscape of Badlands National Park is often compared to the moon's surface. But the area is also home to Buffalo Gap National Grassland, the second largest mixed-grass prairie in the country. The combination of distinct rock formations and lush grasslands makes Badlands one of the most beautiful and bizarre places in the world.

State: South Dakota
Established: November 10, 1978
Size: 244,300 acres (98,865 ha)
Website: nps.gov/badl

DISCOVER BADLANDS

RANGER TIPS

Don't get too close to the edge of any overlooks or trails; the loose ground may erode beneath your feet. Find a fossil? Don't touch it, and report it to the visitor center.

TAKE IT EASY

Go for a walk on the park's many trails (center) or in the mixed-grass prairie, where you'll wander through both ankle-high and waist-high grasses (top).

BE EXTREME

Up for a climb? Parts of the 1.5-mile (2.4-km) round-trip Notch Trail are so steep, you have to scale a log ladder to reach higher ground. Reach the top and be rewarded with sweeping views of the White River Valley Basin.

BEST VIEWS

Head to Big Badlands Overlook for an outstanding aerial view of The Wall and glimpses of the cliffs and grassy prairie (below). The Cliff Shelf Nature Trail also offers a spectacular view of the plains.

ALL ABOUT ANIMALS

Park residents include pronghorn, mule and white-tailed deer, prairie dogs (below), coyotes, butterflies, turtles, snakes, bluebirds, vultures, eagles, and hawks. Bonus points if you spot the once endangered bison, bighorn sheep, swift fox, and black-footed ferret, all species reintroduced to Badlands.

Take a Tour

1 Visit the Ben Reifel Visitor Center (left) for an overview on everything the area has to offer, from its geological past to its current wildlife. Don't miss the film "Land of Stone and Light."

Take a Hike

2 From the Ben Reifel Visitor Center, start down one of the eight nearby trails, which range from easy jaunts to longer treks. You'll walk by Badlands' most amazing formations, like The Wall, a long, narrow spine of buttes (right) stretching for 60 miles (96.6 km).

Take a Drive

3 Situated just ten minutes off the interstate, Badlands is superaccessible by car. Follow the 25-mile (40.2-km) Badlands Loop (left) and watch eroded buttes, pinnacles, spires, and grasslands pass by your window.

44

Look for Fossils

5 Follow the quarter-mile (0.4-km) round-trip Fossil Exhibit Trail and find out about the extinct animals that once roamed the badlands, from three-toed horses to saber-toothed cats (left). If you're lucky, you may be able to watch paleontologists excavate for prehistoric bones.

Watch Wildlife

4 Grab your binoculars and head down Sage Creek Rim Road into the park's wilderness area. You may spot buffalo (left), pronghorn, and bighorn sheep roaming the grasslands.

[DARE TO EXPLORE]

HEADS UP
Two hours from Badlands, near Keystone, South Dakota, looms Mount Rushmore National Memorial, the iconic landmark featuring the heads of four former U.S. presidents carved in the side of a mountain. Take the half-mile (0.8-km)-long Presidential Trail to look up the noses of the presidents and stay until sunset for the lighting ceremony. **nps.gov/moru**

GO CRAZY
Travel two hours from Badlands to Crazy Horse, South Dakota, home to the Crazy Horse Memorial. This mountain-size statue of a Lakota Indian riding a horse has been under construction for more than 60 years and is as long as a cruise ship and taller than a 60-story skyscraper! Visit the Indian Museum of North America and learn to grind corn and make crafts just like the Lakota Indians did. **crazyhorsememorial.org**

FOSSIL FUN
Twenty-six thousand years ago, Columbian and woolly mammoths became trapped in a sinkhole and died. Today, you can visit that spot in Hot Springs, South Dakota, known as Mammoth Site (about 2.5 hours from Badlands). Watch fossils being uncovered, explore a hut made out of mammoth bones, and learn more about prehistoric creatures. **mammothsite.com**

TAKE THE PLUNGE
After you leave Mammoth Site, put on your bathing suit and make a stop at Evans Plunge, a water park filled with water from a natural hot spring. Soak or splash in the warm water or shoot down your choice of three slides. **evansplunge.com**

MY CHECKLIST

- ✓ Drive the Badlands Loop Road.
- ✓ Sign up for a ranger-led program like the Geology Walk or Fossil Talk.
- ✓ Hike one of Badland's best trails, such as the Door Trail or the more strenuous Cliff Shelf Trail.
- ✓ Check out the exhibits at the visitor center.
- ✓ Follow the Fossil Exhibit Trail to learn about the prehistoric creatures that lived in the area.
- ✓ Attend a Night Sky program and view the sparkling night sky through a telescope.
- ✓ Look for wildlife roaming in the prairies.

FAST FACT: Badlands National Park is considered to be one of the world's richest deposits of mammal fossil beds.

45

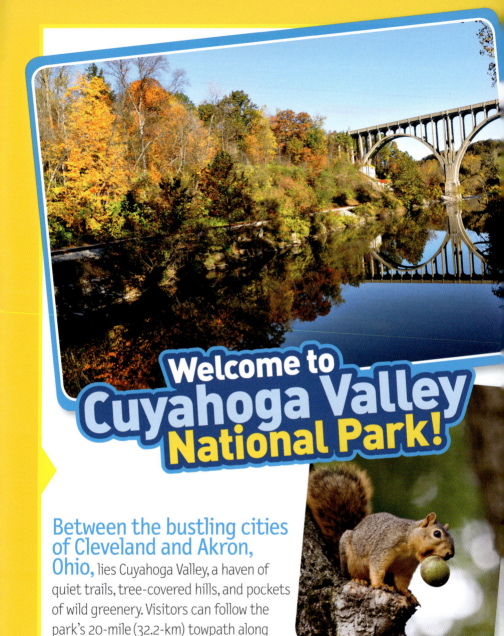

Welcome to Cuyahoga Valley National Park!

SQUIRREL

Between the bustling cities of Cleveland and Akron, Ohio, lies Cuyahoga Valley, a haven of quiet trails, tree-covered hills, and pockets of wild greenery. Visitors can follow the park's 20-mile (32.2-km) towpath along the banks of the Ohio & Erie Canal, spy beavers on the river, gather at a music center for outdoor concerts in the summer, or ride sleds down its hills in the winter. Plus, the park's many waterfalls, abundance of plants, and variety of trees make it one of the region's most beautiful areas—and a true treasure in the state of Ohio.

State: Ohio
Established: October 11, 2000
Size: 33,000 acres (13,355 ha)
Website: nps.gov/cuva

DISCOVER CUYAHOGA VALLEY

BEST VIEWS

Check out Tinkers Creek Gorge, a national natural landmark that offers an overlook with an amazing view of the wooded valley and creek, 200 feet (61 m) below. At dusk, scale Ledges Overlook for stunning and colorful sunset views over wooded ridges as far as the eye can see. For a view of one of the prettiest waterfalls in the park, head down the trail leading to Blue Hen Falls (left).

RANGER TIPS

Ask about ranger-led tours and special events at the Canal Visitor Center. The best times to tour Cuyahoga? Spring (for the wildflowers, right) and fall (for the foliage).

TAKE IT EASY

Hit the trails (below) for a fun and easy adventure or visit the Happy Days Lodge, a center hosting concerts, dances, and kids' activities. Check with the visitor center for a schedule of events. For a step back in time, visit the Hale Farm & Village, where you can see what life was like in the Cuyahoga Valley in the 1800s.

BE EXTREME

Visiting in the winter? Cross-country ski past ponds, down steep hills, and along the Ohio & Erie Canal. You can also opt to sled, snow tube, snowshoe, or downhill ski at nearby resorts. When you're done with your extreme adventure check out the swirling wintertime icicles formed by frozen waterfalls.

ALL ABOUT ANIMALS

The unique urban location of Cuyahoga Valley makes the park a refuge for a variety of animals. Explore the park's trails and wetland habitats to see deer, squirrels, beavers, and birds like the belted kingfisher (below), great blue heron, red-winged blackbird, and bald eagle.

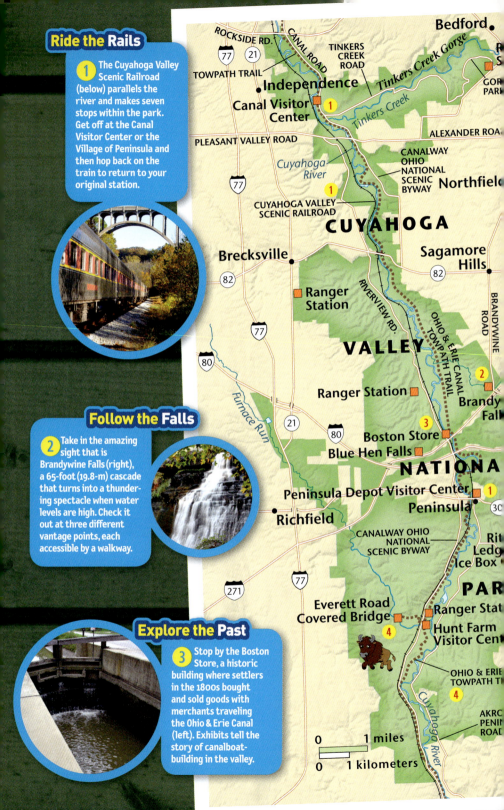

Ride the Rails

1 The Cuyahoga Valley Scenic Railroad (below) parallels the river and makes seven stops within the park. Get off at the Canal Visitor Center or the Village of Peninsula and then hop back on the train to return to your original station.

Follow the Falls

2 Take in the amazing sight that is Brandywine Falls (right), a 65-foot (19.8-m) cascade that turns into a thundering spectacle when water levels are high. Check it out at three different vantage points, each accessible by a walkway.

Explore the Past

3 Stop by the Boston Store, a historic building where settlers in the 1800s bought and sold goods with merchants traveling the Ohio & Erie Canal (left). Exhibits tell the story of canalboat-building in the valley.

48

[DARE TO EXPLORE]

GET WILD
Transport yourself from the forest to the rain forest—and beyond—with a stop at Cleveland Metroparks Zoo & Forest, a 30-minute drive from the park. Be wowed by more than 600 animals and insects from seven continents and a newly opened five-acre (2-ha) elephant exhibit. **clevelandmetroparks.com**

HISTORIC HOUSE
Plan a stop at the James A. Garfield National Historic Site in Mentor, Ohio (about 30 miles [48.3 km] from Cuyahoga). Tour the home of Garfield, the 20th president of the United States, and learn about his life and work. For some quiet time, stroll the home's tranquil grounds and peaceful paths. **nps.gov/jaga**

MUSIC MUSEUM
Spend an afternoon in Cleveland's Rock and Roll Hall of Fame. Dedicated to all things rock and roll, you can listen to music, check out crazy costumes, and see what being a rock star is really like. About 30 minutes from the park. **rockhall.com**

THRILL TIME
Up your thrill factor at Cedar Point, Challenge Park, and Soak City, home to oodles of crazy-fun rides, like the Dragster, a 120-mile-an-hour (193-km/h) roller coaster that zooms 420 feet (128 m) up in the air. In Sandusky, Ohio (about 65 miles [105 km] from Cuyahoga). **cedarpoint.com**

Bike It
4 Pedal along the Ohio & Erie Canal Towpath Trail (below). Shady and flat, the trail rolls for about 20 miles (32.2 km) in the park beside the Cuyahoga River, past marshes, and through the Everett Road Covered Bridge.

Rock Stars
5 Rock 320 million years old forms the 105-foot (32-m)-high Ritchie Ledges (right). Stand in the shadows of these blocks of orange and yellow rock, then explore nearby Ice Box Cave, a 50-foot (15.2-m)-deep narrow slit in the rock where the temperature stays cool year-round.

MY CHECKLIST
- ✓ Stop by the visitor center for fun exhibits and info on the park.
- ✓ Walk or bike the Towpath Trail.
- ✓ Take a ride on the Cuyahoga Valley Scenic Railroad.
- ✓ Visit Lock 38, the last working canal lock within the park.
- ✓ Explore Ritchie Ledges and Ice Box Cave.
- ✓ Climb to the top of Brandywine Falls.
- ✓ In the winter, tour the park by sled, snow tube, skis, or snowshoes.

FAST FACT: This national park is home to more than 60 waterfalls.

49

CENTENNIAL EDITION

GET PACKING!
YOUR NATIONAL PARK SUITCASE CHECKLIST

Packing your suitcase for a national park adventure? Make sure you include these must-haves to ensure a fun-filled trip!

WHAT TO WEAR

Casual and comfy is the dress code, but the weather and activities should dictate what you wear.

➡ WEATHER WATCHER

Before you pack a stitch of clothing, take note of the season and check the weather. Go to the National Park Service website for the park you're visiting (start here: nps.gov), and click on "Things to Know Before You Come." In Death Valley, summer temperatures often reach 120°F (49°C), but in the winter, the lows can be in the 30s (0°C). In Zion National Park, day and nighttime temperatures can easily differ by 30 degrees (17 Celsius degrees).

➡ HAPPY FEET

Walking is a big part of visiting a national park, and keeping your feet dry and warm will make your stay a lot more fun. Bring comfortable shoes and clean, absorbent socks. Consider your planned activities: If you're hiking on trails, closed-toe, comfortable walking shoes are essential—preferably some with gripping soles.

WHAT TO AVOID

A vacation in the national parks means you'll be spending a lot of time outside exposed to the elements. Pack some essentials to avoid these big problems:

➡ SUNBURN

Use a "broad spectrum," water-resistant sunscreen with an SPF of at least 15. Make sure to reapply every two hours.

➡ SUN GLARE

UV-protected sunglasses will guard your eyes from glare and wind.

➡ BUG BITES

Many parks, like the Everglades, get buggy. The best way to avoid getting bitten is to cover up—wear pants and long sleeves. Your parents may want to pack insect repellent. They'll need to read and follow the directions and apply it to you properly. Insect repellent shouldn't be used around your eyes, mouth, or hands.

➡ THIRST AND HUNGER

Bring along a reusable water bottle to make sure you drink enough fluids. Also bring some healthy snacks, such as trail mix, to keep up your energy. Remember not to leave your trash in the park. Take it home and dispose of it responsibly.

WHAT TO DO

Bringing along a few key things can open up a wide range of activities to do in the parks.

➤ SNAP A SHOT: A Camera

Nothing quite lends itself to a postcard-worthy shot like a national park landscape. Pack a camera, along with extra batteries, a fresh memory card, and a tripod if you have one. If you're snapping from your phone, make sure you clear some memory to hold all the photos and video you plan to take. For a little inspiration, check out the official account of the park you're visiting on Instagram.

➤ TAKE A CLOSER LOOK: Binoculars

To get an up-close look at what's around you, bring along a pair of binoculars. If you're in Yosemite Valley, look for rock climbers scaling El Capitan from the meadow at the base of the rock formation. Binoculars are also handy for birding and spotting other wildlife from a safe distance.

➤ MAKE A PLAN: Maps

One of the best parts about traveling to a new place is the excitement of getting ready. You can be your family's in-house expert on landmarks! Spend some time studying a park map—either in this guidebook or ones from the National Park Service website—to learn the names of trails and roads, and to learn where the visitor centers are.

➤ PLAY A GAME: Checklists

Research the wildlife you might see, and create checklists for your family. For example, if you're headed to Yellowstone, create a checklist by drawing, say, a bison, bear, wolf, and elk, then putting a box next to them. When you're in the park, check off the animals as you see them, and compare your drawing to the real thing. You can make the same kind of checklist for seashells, trees, marine life, rocks, leaves, and animal tracks for other parks.

➤ BE INSPIRED: A Pen and Paper

Bring a pen and journal along so you can make notes about your observations of the national parks' landscapes and features. Maybe you'll be inspired to write a journal entry describing your day, a poem, or some song lyrics. If you're having a rest on the trail in the Great Smoky Mountains, pull out your journal and sketch what you see. Or describe the sounds you hear, or the scent of the forest.

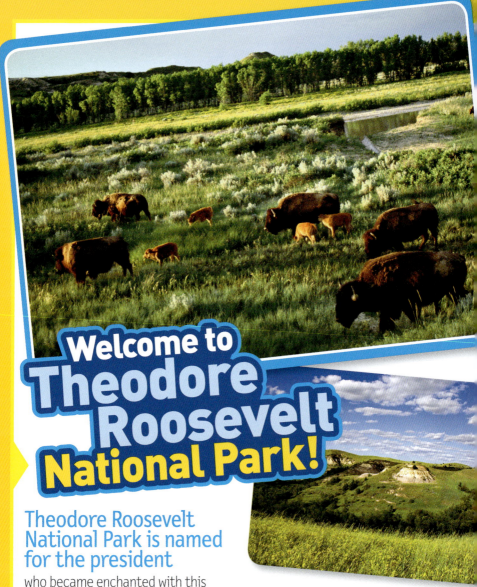

Welcome to Theodore Roosevelt National Park!

Theodore Roosevelt National Park is named for the president who became enchanted with this unique area back in 1883—and then went on to establish five national parks and help found the U.S. Forest Service. Known for its rugged terrain, the park began forming its unique landscape 65 million years ago. Today the park is home to a rich variety of wildlife and includes both the Little Missouri River and the Little Missouri badlands; it is divided into two parts (the South and North Units). Its unrivaled array of jagged cliffs, steep slopes, rounded hills, and springtime wildflowers spreading vivid colors throughout the prairies makes Theodore Roosevelt a one-of-a-kind destination.

State: North Dakota
Established: November 10, 1978
Size: 70,447 acres (28,509 ha)
Website: nps.gov/thro

DISCOVER THEODORE ROOSEVELT

RANGER TIPS

Keep your distance from bison; they are quick and may attack if approached. Make sure to also keep an eye out for rattlesnakes and black widow spiders, which often live in prairie dog burrows. And don't feed the prairie dogs—they bite!

TAKE IT EASY

On clear nights, you can *almost* see forever (above). So head to the park after dark, lie back, and look for planets, stars, constellations, and maybe even a meteor shower!

BE EXTREME

Hop on a horse and gallop down some of the Maah Daah Hey Trail (above), which at one point crosses over the Little Missouri River.

BEST VIEWS

In the South Unit, pull off at the North Dakota Badlands Overlook for an amazing look at the area around you. In the North Unit, the River Bend Overlook offers a stunning vista of the Little Missouri River (below) and badlands on either side.

ALL ABOUT ANIMALS

Look for prairie dogs (below) along the Scenic Loop Drive (and listen for their telltale chirp as they warn each other of your arrival). You may also see beavers in the river and white-tailed deer, bison, elk, antelope, and wild horses grazing on the grassy plateaus. And watch for birds, too. There are more than 180 types of birds that either live in or pass through the park!

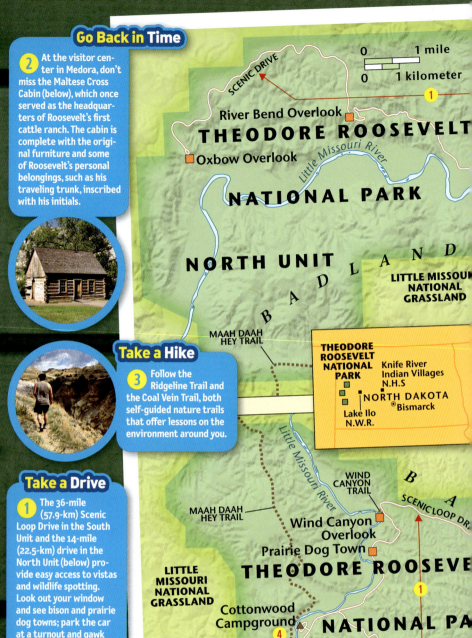

Go Back in Time

2 At the visitor center in Medora, don't miss the Maltese Cross Cabin (below), which once served as the headquarters of Roosevelt's first cattle ranch. The cabin is complete with the original furniture and some of Roosevelt's personal belongings, such as his traveling trunk, inscribed with his initials.

Take a Hike

3 Follow the Ridgeline Trail and the Coal Vein Trail, both self-guided nature trails that offer lessons on the environment around you.

Take a Drive

1 The 36-mile (57.9-km) Scenic Loop Drive in the South Unit and the 14-mile (22.5-km) drive in the North Unit (below) provide easy access to vistas and wildlife spotting. Look out your window and see bison and prairie dog towns; park the car at a turnout and gawk at the amazingly unique landscape.

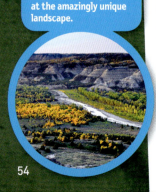

54

[DARE TO EXPLORE]

GO TO THE GRASSLAND
Spot more wildlife at the Little Missouri National Grassland, where bighorn sheep, elk, pronghorn, hawks, and grouse live. You can also camp, hike, and horseback ride in this protected prairie surrounding Theodore Roosevelt National Park. **www.fs.usda.gov/dpg/**

SEEK REFUGE
Boat, fish, picnic, and take in stunning sights at Lake Ilo National Wildlife Refuge, about 50 miles (80.5 km) east of Theodore Roosevelt National Park. **fws.gov/lakeilo**

PLAY TIME
Make believe you're back in the Wild West at Medora Children's Park. Play in an Old West fort, a stagecoach, and an old-fashioned train engine. Located near the national park's headquarters in Medora. **medora.com**

GO TRIBAL
Make a stop at the Knife River Indian Villages National Historic Site, about 130 miles (209 km) east of Theodore Roosevelt. You'll see the remains of Native American villages, once home to thriving civilizations. An on-site museum highlights the colorful culture of the local tribes that have lived on the land for more than 11,000 years. **nps.gov/knri**

Camp Out
4 Pitch a tent in Cottonwood Campground, near the banks of the Little Missouri River, which winds through Wind Canyon (right). Plopped in the middle of the wilderness, you're bound to have a close encounter with wildlife ... and just may wake up in the morning to find bison tracks outside your site.

Family Fun
5 Head to the South Unit Visitor Center to borrow a Family Fun Pack. For 24 hours, you'll be loaned field guides, binoculars, hand lenses, and activities to help make your visit even more exciting.

MY CHECKLIST
- ✓ Check out Roosevelt's belongings at the Maltese Cross Cabin.
- ✓ Go on a bike ride on one of the park's paved or dirt roads.
- ✓ Hike some of the many self-guided trails in the park.
- ✓ Take in a view of the Little Missouri River.
- ✓ Soak in the sights from the car on the drive along Scenic Loop.
- ✓ Sleep under the stars at Cottonwood Campground.
- ✓ Pick up a Family Fun Pack at the South Unit Visitor Center.

FAST FACT: Fifty-five million years ago, the Dakota plains were a swamp similar to southern Louisiana.

55

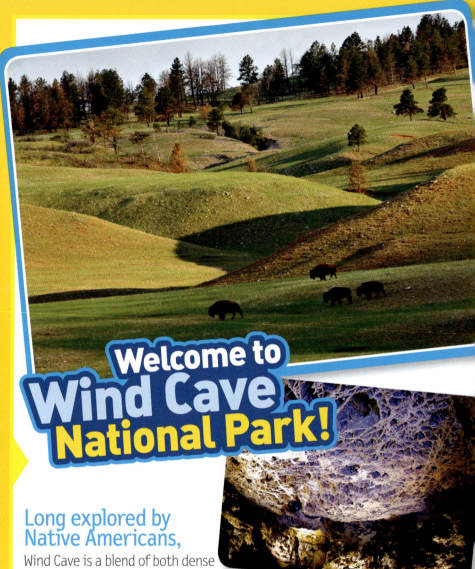

Welcome to Wind Cave National Park!

Long explored by Native Americans, Wind Cave is a blend of both dense woods and wide-open grasslands. But the true gem of this park is actually something you can't see—unless you travel underground. Discovered by two brothers in 1881, Wind Cave features 140 miles (225 km) of underground passages, making it one of the world's longest caves.

In the caves, you will see many bizarre mineral formations, including honeycomb-like structures called boxwork. Listen closely and you just may hear a whistling noise—that's the sound of the strong winds that rush in and out of the cave's mouth, giving the park its name.

State: South Dakota
Established: January 9, 1903
Size: 33,847 acres (13,697 ha)
Website: nps.gov/wica

DISCOVER WIND CAVE

RANGER TIPS

Don't rely on cell phones to stay in touch; coverage is spotty within Wind Cave. You should also be prepared for severe thunderstorms and occasional hail, most common in the summer. And bring a light sweater or jacket: The caves are only 53°F (12°C) year-round.

TAKE IT EASY

Need a break? Grab some snacks, spread out a blanket, and relax at the designated picnic areas near the visitor center and Elk Mountain Campground. If you're in the mood for a walk, enjoy the beautiful rolling prairies (top) or take the Garden of Eden cave tour, an easy one-hour loop. (Note: There is a fee for the tour.)

BE EXTREME

Delve deep into Wind Cave on the four-hour Wild Cave Tour (below). Crawl through narrow openings, squeeze into tight passages, and get dirty as you scramble into the far reaches of this massive cave. (Note: The minimum age for the Wild Cave Tour is 16, and the park requires a signed consent form for those 17 and under.)

BEST VIEW

From the Rankin Ridge Trail, walk the one-mile (1.6-km) loop among the Ponderosa pines (above) to a fire tower. You can climb partway up the tower for a great view of the surrounding landscape.

ALL ABOUT ANIMALS

Take a walk around and you're bound to see pronghorn (below), mule deer, and prairie dogs scampering about in the open grasslands. Bison also roam here. And because of the park's small size and relatively large bison population, your chances of seeing them are pretty good! Also look for elk (you might spot some on the outer edges of the forests), red-tailed hawks, golden eagles, bats, insects, and fish.

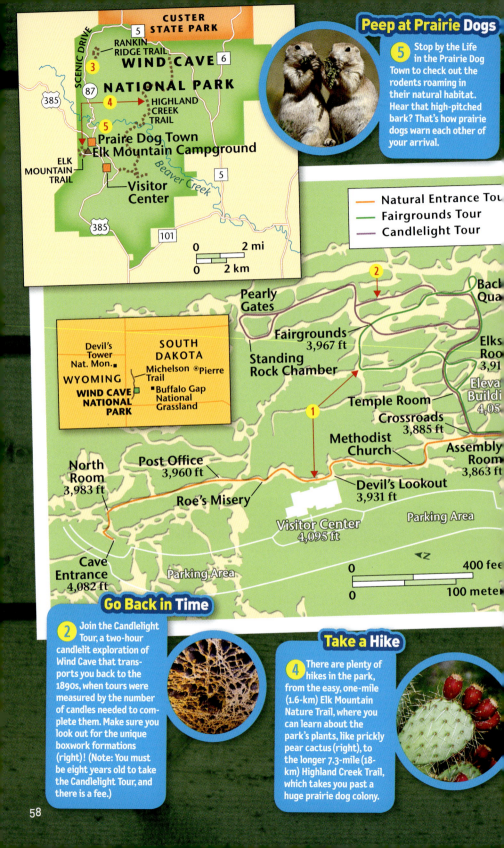

Peep at Prairie Dogs

5 Stop by the Life in the Prairie Dog Town to check out the rodents roaming in their natural habitat. Hear that high-pitched bark? That's how prairie dogs warn each other of your arrival.

Go Back in Time

2 Join the Candlelight Tour, a two-hour candlelit exploration of Wind Cave that transports you back to the 1890s, when tours were measured by the number of candles needed to complete them. Make sure you look out for the unique boxwork formations (right)! (Note: You must be eight years old to take the Candlelight Tour, and there is a fee.)

Take a Hike

4 There are plenty of hikes in the park, from the easy, one-mile (1.6-km) Elk Mountain Nature Trail, where you can learn about the park's plants, like prickly pear cactus (right), to the longer 7.3-mile (18-km) Highland Creek Trail, which takes you past a huge prairie dog colony.

[DARE TO EXPLORE]

PARK HOP
Take time to visit the adjacent Custer State Park. The 1,300-strong bison herd is one of the largest in the world. Also nearby? Buffalo Gap National Grassland (about 75 miles [121 km] from Wind Cave), where you can hike, mountain bike, or camp among the mix of grasslands and badlands.
gfp.sd.gov/state-parks/directory/custer (Custer); **(605) 279-2125** (Buffalo Gap)

EXPLORE MORE
Can't get enough of caving? Travel to Custer, South Dakota, about 35 miles (56.3 km) northwest of Wind Cave, to see Jewel Cave National Monument. This 173-mile (278-km)-long cave features calcite crystals that sparkle like jewels.
(605) 673-2288; nps.gov/jeca

TERRIFIC TOWER
Make your way to Devils Tower, which became the country's first national monument in 1906. Rising 1,267 feet (386 m) above the Belle Fourche River, you can explore the tower—and the surrounding park packed with plenty of plants and wildlife. Located in Devils Tower, Wyoming, about 130 miles (209 km) from Wind Cave. **nps.gov/deto**

TOP TRAIL
Bike or hike down the George S. Mickelson Trail, in the heart of the Black Hills. Pass through national forestland, over railroad bridges and through four rock tunnels. Or opt to take the trolley on the trail, a four-hour ride along the 109-mile (175-km) path.
gfp.sd.gov/state-parks/directory/mickelson-trail

Take a Tour

1 Stop by the visitor center to watch the film "Wind Cave: One Park, Two Worlds," which narrates details about the park's history and unusual ecosystem. From there, you can take the Natural Entrance Tour or the Fairgrounds Tour—both introduce you to the underground world of caves.

Take a Drive

3 Explore the park's prairies and forests from your car by following the Scenic Drive. See some stunning views, spot bison and pronghorn grazing on grass, and stop at one of the many pullouts to learn more about the park's ecology.

MY CHECKLIST
- ✓ Explore Wind Cave.
- ✓ Stop by the visitor center to learn about cave exploration.
- ✓ Join a ranger-led tour.
- ✓ Take a scenic drive to see all of the sights.
- ✓ Camp out at Elk Mountain Campground.
- ✓ Look for wildlife roaming the park's grassy plains.
- ✓ Stay past sunset to stargaze or join in the nightly campfire talk.

FAST FACT: Wind Cave is the world's fourth largest cave.

CENTENNIAL EDITION

THE NATIONAL PARK AWESOME EIGHT

National parks are filled with animals often not seen in other parts of the country, because the parks provide protected habitats, allowing them to thrive. Here are some wildly weird facts about eight national park critters.

AMERICAN CROCODILE

FOUND IN: Florida's Everglades and Biscayne National Parks

GETTING WEIRD: American crocodiles swallow small rocks to help digest their food and control their buoyancy in the water.

GRIZZLY BEAR

FOUND IN: Yellowstone, Glacier, Grand Teton, and North Cascades, as well as in many Alaska national parks

GETTING WEIRD: Grizzly bears may look large and slow-moving, but they can run up to 35 miles an hour (56 km/h). That's about twice as fast as your cruising speed on a bike!

PRONGHORN

FOUND IN: Yellowstone, Grand Teton, Wind Cave, Petrified Forest, and Great Basin National Parks, along with Organ Pipe Cactus National Monument

GETTING WEIRD: Pronghorn are the second fastest mammal on Earth—just behind the cheetah—and can reach speeds of 53 miles an hour (86 km/h)!

MANATEE

FOUND IN: Florida's Everglades and Biscayne National Parks, and Canaveral National Seashore

GETTING WEIRD: These gentle giants of seas and rivers weigh up to 1,300 pounds (600 kg)—that's as much as the combined weight of 18 golden retrievers!

BALD EAGLE

FOUND IN: National parks with especially good viewing include Crater Lake, Glacier Bay, Olympic National Park, and Acadia. Thanks to recovery efforts, the bald eagle is considered "recovered" in the U.S. except in the Sonoran Desert.

GETTING WEIRD: The bald eagle—the national bird of the U.S.—is a fierce competitor for a meal. It will steal a fish right out of another bird's talons! Benjamin Franklin once said he thought the bald eagle had "bad moral character" and thought the wild turkey was a bird more worthy of the national emblem.

AMERICAN BISON

FOUND IN: Wyoming's Yellowstone National Park

GETTING WEIRD: American bison are massive. They weigh up to 2,000 pounds (907 kg)—more than twice as heavy as a concert grand piano. And their thick coat is so insulated, snow can settle on their back and it won't melt!

MOOSE

FOUND IN: National parks in Alaska, Washington, Colorado, Minnesota, Michigan, and Maine

GETTING WEIRD: Moose are excellent swimmers. They can paddle for several miles at a time and can dive underwater for up to 30 seconds!

BIGHORN SHEEP

FOUND IN: Rocky Mountain and Yellowstone National Parks

GETTING WEIRD: The epic battles of male Rocky Mountain bighorn sheep are straight out of an action movie. Fighting for dominance, males run at a 20-mile-an-hour (32-km/h) charge and clash horns repeatedly, sometimes for hours until one walks away. Their thick skull generally prevents injuries.

⏩ Other Must-see Park Properties in the Midwest

 AGATE FOSSIL BEDS NATIONAL MONUMENT (NE)

nps.gov/agfo

WHY IT'S COOL: It's an essential site for the study of ancient mammals and Native American artifacts.

WHAT TO DO: View the Cook Collection of American Indian Artifacts and the fossils of ancient mammals, hike the Niobrara River Valley.

TRY THIS: Hike to the top of 40-foot (12.2-m)-high Agate Falls on the middle branch of the Ontonagon River.

APOSTLE ISLANDS NATIONAL LAKESHORE (WI)

nps.gov/apis

WHY IT'S COOL: You won't believe the beauty of the park's 21 Lake Superior islands and 12 miles (19.3 km) of shoreline.

WHAT TO DO: Visit historic lighthouses; hiking, boating, sailing, cruising, camping, fishing, and scuba diving.

TRY THIS: Launch a kayak from Meyers Beach and explore mainland sea caves.

ICE AGE NATIONAL SCENIC TRAIL (WI)

nps.gov/iatr

WHY IT'S COOL: The trail traces the edge of an ancient glacier, offering views of cool geological formations.

WHAT TO DO: Hiking, backpacking, camping, bird-watching, stargazing, and snowshoeing.

TRY THIS: Visiting in the winter? Strap on some cross-country skis and hit some of the park's 1,200 miles (1,931 km) of trails.

JEFFERSON NATIONAL EXPANSION MEMORIAL (MO)

nps.gov/jeff

WHY IT'S COOL: Its centerpiece is the 630-foot (192-m)-tall Gateway Arch in St. Louis, the tallest man-made monument in the United States.

WHAT TO DO: Visit the arch, explore the riverfront area by bike, and visit the Museum of Westward Expansion.

TRY THIS: Take a tram ride to the top of the arch for sweeping views of the St. Louis area.

LEWIS & CLARK NATIONAL HISTORIC TRAIL (IL, MO, KS, IA, NE, SD, ND, MT, ID, OR, WA)

nps.gov/lecl

WHY IT'S COOL: It's the route taken by the Lewis and Clark expedition in its search for a water route to the Pacific Ocean between 1804 and 1806.

WHAT TO DO: Retrace the expedition's path by car, bicycle, or boat; skiing or snowshoeing in the winter; rafting or canoeing the Missouri River.

TRY THIS: Hike Idaho's Bitterroot Mountains in the footsteps of early American explorers.

MISSISSIPPI NATIONAL RIVER AND RECREATION AREA (MN)

nps.gov/miss

WHY IT'S COOL: This 72-mile (116-km) stretch of America's iconic river is home to St. Anthony Falls (the Mississippi's only major waterfall) and Stone Arch Bridge (a national engineering landmark).

WHAT TO DO: Visit museums and historic sites; boating, canoeing, hiking, biking, camping, picnicking, wildlife-watching, cross-country skiing, and snowshoeing.

TRY THIS: Hop on a bike and ride a portion of the 3,000-mile (4,828-km)-long Mississippi River Trail.

MOUNT RUSHMORE NATIONAL MEMORIAL (SD)

nps.gov/moru

WHY IT'S COOL: It features huge sculptures of the heads of former U.S. presidents.

WHAT TO DO: Go on a ranger-led walk to the base of the carving, then take a Sculptor's Studio Tour to check out the cool tools they use.

TRY THIS: Visit nearby Jewel Cave (the third longest cave in the world) to see cool cave formations.

OZARK NATIONAL SCENIC RIVERWAYS NATIONAL RIVER (MO)

nps.gov/ozar

WHY IT'S COOL: Home to two of America's clearest and most beautiful spring-fed rivers, it's also the first national park area to protect a wild river system.

WHAT TO DO: Watch traditional Ozarks craft and skills demonstrations; canoeing, kayaking, inner-tubing, hiking, and horseback riding.

TRY THIS: Explore life beneath the Earth's surface at Ozark Caverns in Lake of the Ozarks State Park.

PICTURED ROCKS NATIONAL LAKESHORE (MI)

nps.gov/piro

WHY IT'S COOL: It offers natural beauty along 40 miles (64.4 km) of Lake Superior shoreline, including waterfalls, cliffs, beaches, and sand dunes.

WHAT TO DO: Visit the Grand Sable Banks and Dunes; view the Pictured Rocks; hiking, camping, backpacking, bicycling, boating, kayaking, skiing, and snowmobiling.

TRY THIS: On a hot day, take a chilly dip in the clean and clear waters of Lake Superior or just hang out on the lakeshore's white-sand beaches.

SLEEPING BEAR DUNES NATIONAL LAKESHORE (MI)

nps.gov/slbe

WHY IT'S COOL: Thirty-five miles (56.3 km) of Lake Michigan coastline plus the North and South Manitou Islands make up this site.

WHAT TO DO: Visit the U.S. Coast Guard Museum; check out the South Manitou Island Lighthouse; tour historic sites; swimming, hiking, kayaking, and canoeing.

TRY THIS: Climb the Sleeping Bear Dunes, check out views of Glen Lake, then run down to the picnic area to recharge before you climb again.

TALLGRASS PRAIRIE NATIONAL PRESERVE (KS)

nps.gov/tapr

WHY IT'S COOL: It protects a remnant of the threatened tallgrass prairie.

WHAT TO DO: Hiking, wildlife-watching, and fishing.

TRY THIS: Tour the preserve's backcountry while learning about the prairie's plants, animals, and geology on a ranger-led prairie bus tour.

Carlsbad Caverns National Park

Stunning stalactite formations cover the ceiling of an underground chamber in Carlsbad Caverns.

the Southwest

the Southwest

THOUSANDS OF YEARS AGO, an ancient sea sculpted the landscapes of the Southwest. This resulted in a wide range of dazzling scenery seen in the Southwest's national parks, including amazing mountain chains, cool dark caverns, dramatic canyons, a flowing river, and rolling dunes of sand. With such diversity to its landscapes, the Southwest holds the potential for plenty of fun wherever you go, whether hiking a mountain trail, shooting down river rapids, exploring canyons and caves, or taking a spin along one of the area's many scenic drives.

Depending on the yearly precipitation, the Southwest is either awash with brilliant blossoms, like the gorgeous Texas bluebonnets, red and orange cactus flowers, and white yucca blooms, or covered by cacti and other plants that thrive in a parched terrain, like the prickly pear.

This varied climate and topography brings a world of wildlife to the Southwest; it's not unusual to see lizards skittering or snakes slithering along the many trails dissecting the parks. In fact, animals have been roaming this land long before humans, as evident in the many dinosaur fossils found by paleontologists in the Southwest, including the Big Bend pterosaur, the largest animal ever to fly.

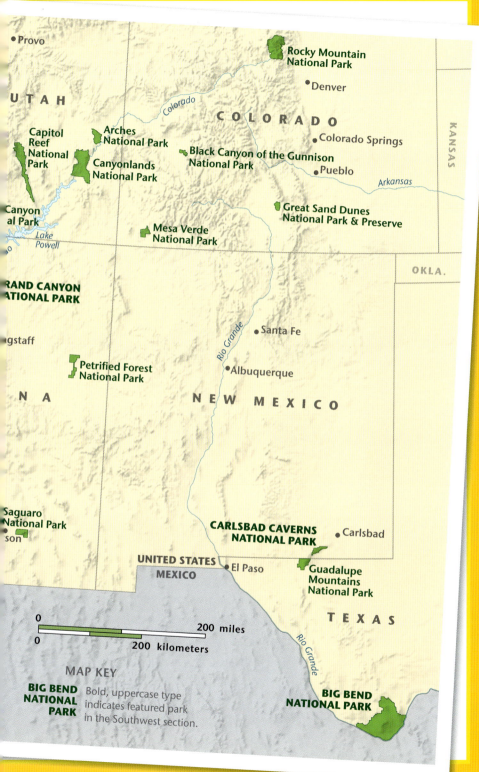

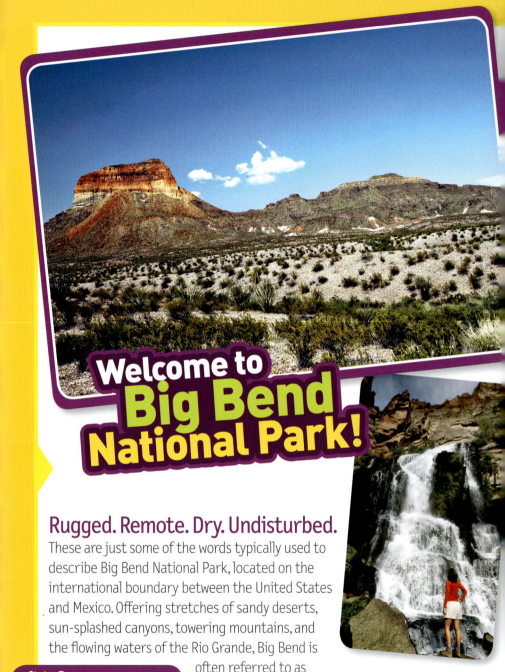

Welcome to Big Bend National Park!

Rugged. Remote. Dry. Undisturbed.

These are just some of the words typically used to describe Big Bend National Park, located on the international boundary between the United States and Mexico. Offering stretches of sandy deserts, sun-splashed canyons, towering mountains, and the flowing waters of the Rio Grande, Big Bend is often referred to as "three parks in one." The wide range of landscape offers many trails, a variety of wildlife, and photo ops everywhere you roam. So regardless of how remote Big Bend may be, you'll always have plenty to keep you occupied—and amazed.

State: Texas
Established: June 12, 1944
Size: 801,163 acres (324,220 ha)
Website: nps.gov/bibe

DISCOVER BIG BEND

RANGER TIPS

The sun is strong in Big Bend and the weather is unpredictable. Stay hydrated, wear sunscreen and a hat, and bring clothes for different climates.

TAKE IT EASY

Take a leisurely float trip along the Rio Grande through tranquil Boquillas Canyon. A half-day trip lets you explore the park's canyons while kicking back in a raft or heading out on the river in a canoe (right). If you prefer dry land, visit the Rio Grande Village and do some bird-watching. With more than 450 species counted, Big Bend is home to more bird species than any other national park!

BE EXTREME

"Run" the Rio Grande with a professionally trained white-water-rapid guide (below). Hit Colorado, Contrabando, and Mariscal Canyons—all offering Class 2 and 3 rapids. Check in with the visitor center for details.

BEST VIEWS

If you're up for a longer hike, head up to South Rim (13 miles [20.9 km] round trip) or Emory Peak (10.5 miles [16.9 km] round trip), two of the highest points in the park providing views of pretty much everything in Big Bend (above). Not up for the trek? Drive to the Rio Grande Overlook to see vistas of the Sierra del Carmen, the river floodplain, and part of a village in Mexico. If you're visiting in the springtime, you'll also get beautiful views of Big Bend's blooming bluebonnets.

ALL ABOUT ANIMALS

The desert, the mountains, and the river provide habitats for a dizzying array of animals, such as bats, birds (like this western scrub-jay), snakes, lizards, turtles, fish, mountain lions, and bears.

Camp Out

5 Pitch a tent at one of the campgrounds scattered throughout Big Bend National Park. Just be prepared to get rugged: The campgrounds do not offer electricity and fuel.

Take a Hike

2 Explore Big Bend's wilderness on one of the many hiking trails in the park, like this one in Boquillas Canyon (right). Select a trail according to your skill level (the Window View Trail and Chihuahuan Desert Nature Trail are easy but picturesque), then enjoy the awesome sights around you.

Take a Drive

1 Stay in the car and hit the Ross Maxwell Scenic Drive, which winds through the Chihuahuan Desert, past the park's unique rock formations and other highlights, like Mule Ears Viewpoint and Tuff Canyon. Want to venture even further in? Access extremely remote backcountry roads in a guided jeep tour.

Pedal On

3 Big Bend's roads are perfect for pedaling. Mountain bikers have 150 miles (241 km) of backcountry roads to pick from, while those who prefer smoother journeys can tour the park's 100 miles (161 km) of paved roads. Either way, you'll have a ride with a view.

Dino Drive

4 Take a break on the drive from the Persimmon Gap Visitor Center to the Panther Junction Visitor Center and check out Big Bend's prehistoric past. The roadside Fossil Bone Exhibit shows replica dinosaur bones found in the park, with a larger exhibit coming soon.

[DARE TO EXPLORE]

WALK THROUGH HISTORY
From 1854 to 1891, Fort Davis served as a military post and a place where thousands of emigrants and travelers sought protection prior to the Civil War. Today, you can explore this national historic site and learn more about what life was like way back when. Located in Fort Davis, Texas, about 140 miles (225 km) from Big Bend. **nps.gov/foda**

PARK HOP
Continue your tour of southwest Texas at Big Bend Ranch State Park, adjacent to the national park. Spy longhorn cattle; hike, bike, or ride a horse on some of the park's 66 miles (106 km) of trails; or raft along the 23 miles (37 km) of the Rio Grande managed by Big Bend Ranch. It's also home to one of Madrid Falls, the second highest waterfall in Texas. **tpwd.texas.gov/state-parks/big-bend-ranch**

BE A STAR
Love to stargaze? Head to the McDonald Observatory in the Davis Mountains, about 160 miles (257 km) from Big Bend. Home to one of the world's largest optical telescopes, the observatory offers you a chance to explore the night sky while learning all about the planets and solar system. **mcdonaldobservatory.org**

MY CHECKLIST

✓ Stop at the park's visitor centers for fun exhibits and important info.

✓ Follow a nature trail and enjoy the surroundings.

✓ Take a ranger-guided hike or a workshop.

✓ Head to Boquillas Canyon for a fun and easy river float.

✓ Explore the park by car—either my own or in a guided jeep tour.

✓ Hike or bike the park's trails.

✓ Sleep under the stars at one of the park's campgrounds.

FAST FACT: "Big Bend" refers to the sharp turn the Rio Grande takes in this area.

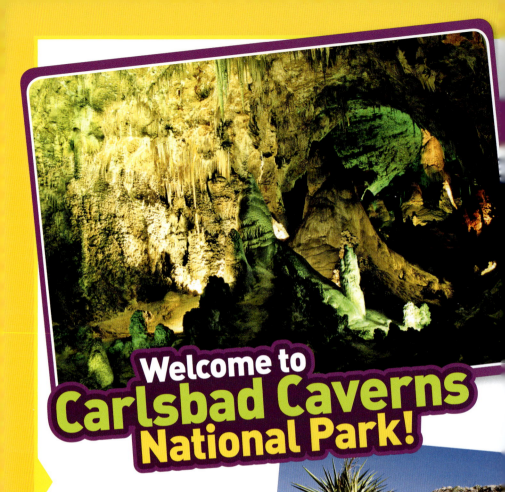

Welcome to Carlsbad Caverns National Park!

When you enter Carlsbad Caverns National Park

you see acres of rugged terrain, rocky slopes, and wide canyons. What don't you see? The 119 caves carved deep below the Earth's surface, formed millions of years ago. These caverns are open for exploration, where visitors are wowed by giant stalagmites and stalactites, reflective pools, and other funky formations. Above ground, you can camp out and hike among the park's vast deserts and canyons, where many mammals and reptiles roam and cacti stretch their spiny arms to the sky.

State: New Mexico
Established: May 14, 1930
Size: 46,766 acres (18,926 ha)
Website: nps.gov/cave

DISCOVER CARLSBAD CAVERNS

RANGER TIPS

Visit between spring and late fall to see the Mexican free-tailed bats (right) hanging out in the caves. The temperature underground is about 56°F (13°C), so make sure to bring a light jacket to stay warm. And stay sturdy on your feet in the caves by wearing comfy shoes with good traction.

TAKE IT EASY

Relax at Rattlesnake Springs picnic area, about 15 miles (24.1 km) from the visitor center. Play in the grass or lie under the shade of the large cottonwood trees.

BE EXTREME

Tour Slaughter Canyon Cave for a more "off-road" caving experience and take in the cool formations, such as helictites (below). There is no paved path on this tour, and the only light is from your flashlight.

BEST VIEWS

One of the park's most magnificent views is in the parking area. High above an ancient reef, you can see a striking vista of the ancient seabed and, on a clear day, 100 miles (161 km) away into Texas.

ALL ABOUT ANIMALS

Besides the abundance of bats, you may also spot mammals like mule deer, mountain lion, black bear, and the Chihuahuan Desert pocket mouse (center), which was not documented in the park until the 21st century. There are also 46 species of reptiles here, including the gray-banded kingsnake (below), the Rio Grande cooter turtle, and the mottled rock rattlesnake.

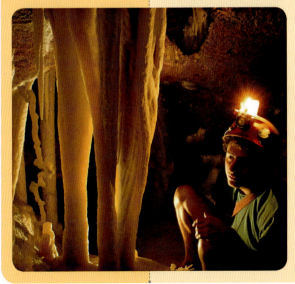

Go Caving

2 A trip to Carlsbad Caverns (below) is not complete without a look at its caves, which start at 750 feet (229 m) below the Earth's surface. Hike or take an elevator down to the eight-acre (3.2-ha) Big Room (where there is a lunch room), then take a guided tour or explore the caverns on your own. Must-see sights? Giant Dome (a 62-foot [18.9-km] stalagmite) and the 140-foot (46.7-m)-deep Bottomless Pit.

Take a Drive

1 The park's Walnut Canyon Desert Drive is a scenic, seven-mile (11.3-km) gravel loop that takes you along a ridge to Rattlesnake Canyon, then back to the visitor center through upper Walnut Canyon (right).

Bat Watch

3 From May to October, you can watch nearly 400,000 Mexican free-tailed bats (below) leave Carlsbad Caverns at dusk to feed on insects at the Pecos River. Watch this sensational sight from the park amphitheater (check at the visitor center for the exact time and details).

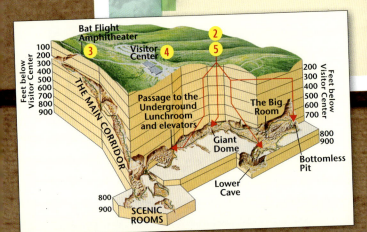

Just for Kids

4 Visiting in the summer? Sign up for KidsCorner at the visitor center to learn about bats, caves, plants, and animals of the desert, like the Mexican squirrel (left). You'll also participate in a fun crafts activity or a game.

[DARE TO EXPLORE]

SMOKEY'S HOME
Back in 1950, a game warden in Lincoln National Forest rescued a black bear cub from a forest fire and named him Smokey Bear—who became the famous symbol of fire prevention. Visit this massive forest, adjacent to Carlsbad Caverns National Park, offering 370 campsites, hiking trails, and plenty of places to picnic. **www.fs.usda.gov/lincoln**

DUNE IT
Want to see some of the world's largest sand dunes? Check out White Sands National Monument, a whopping 275-square-mile (712-sq-km) desert about 190 miles (306 km) from Carlsbad National Park. **nps.gov/whsa**

FIND FOSSILS
Go on a fossil hunt in Guadalupe Mountains National Park, featuring a rocky landscape loaded with the bones of prehistoric creatures. **nps.gov/gumo**

EXPLORE MORE
Learn about life in the Chihuahuan Desert at Living Desert Zoo and Gardens State Park, featuring 40 native animal species and hundreds of native cacti and plants. **www.emnrd.state .nm.us/SPD/livingdesertstatepark.html**

Take a Tour

5 If you opt for a guided tour, consider the King's Palace tour, a 1.5-hour journey to the deepest portion of the cavern open to the public, 830 feet (253 m) beneath the desert surface. Look for helictites, draperies, columns (left), and soda straws. Another highlight? The Left Hand Tunnel Tour, a lantern-lit tour highlighting Carlsbad Caverns' history, formations, cave pools, and fossils. Check at the visitor center for details. (Note: The King's Palace is for ages four and over, and the Left Hand Tunnel is for ages six and over.)

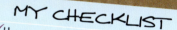

MY CHECKLIST
✓ Have a picnic under the cottonwood trees at Rattlesnake Springs.
✓ Stop at the visitor center to learn all about the park.
✓ Take in the park's awesome outside views before heading underground.
✓ Watch Mexican free-tailed bats fly out of caves.
✓ Take a cave tour and check out the cool underground sights.
✓ Enjoy the views from scenic Walnut Canyon Desert Drive.
✓ Experience the lantern-lit tour and check out the Big Room.

FAST FACT: An ancient inland sea formed Carlsbad Caverns over 250 million years ago.

75

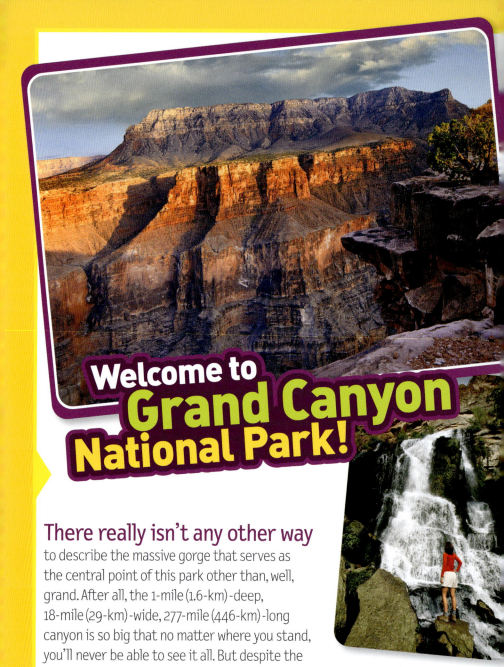

Welcome to Grand Canyon National Park!

There really isn't any other way to describe the massive gorge that serves as the central point of this park other than, well, grand. After all, the 1-mile (1.6-km)-deep, 18-mile (29-km)-wide, 277-mile (446-km)-long canyon is so big that no matter where you stand, you'll never be able to see it all. But despite the magnet-like draw of the main canyon (nearly six million people visit each year), the three areas of this park also offer trails through cool evergreen forests, a winding river, gurgling streams, cascading waterfalls, and phenomenal views.

State: Arizona
Established: February 26, 1919
Size: 1,217,403 acres (492,666 ha)
Website: nps.gov/grca

DISCOVER GRAND CANYON

RANGER TIPS

Be careful standing near the rim of the canyon, especially when you're trying to get that perfect picture, and carry water at all times—it gets hot!

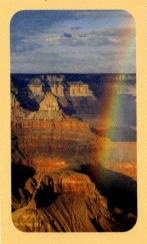

BE EXTREME

Take a river trip through a canyon on the Colorado River (below). Whether you take a day-long tour or one that lasts a week, make sure you're ready for a wet and bumpy ride! Want more adventure? Try Rim Trail, which goes from the canyon's edge for about 13 miles (20.9 km) from Pipe Creek Vista to Hermits Rest (a limestone building on the canyon's rim). Note: The path is only paved until you reach Maricopa Point, then it becomes a dirt trail, a part of which is steep. If you get tired, you can always pick up a shuttle bus at any of the main overlooks or at the end of the trail.

BEST VIEW

Check out the Desert View Watchtower, the highest point on the South Rim, featuring views of the Grand Canyon (top), the Painted Desert to the east, and the San Francisco Peaks to the south. Mather Point is another must-see stop, offering a panoramic view into the heart of the Grand Canyon.

ALL ABOUT ANIMALS

Grand Canyon is home to 89 types of mammals, 65 kinds of reptiles and amphibians, 17 species of fish, and more than 300 different birds! Look for bighorn sheep, mule deer, mountain lions, bobcats, coyotes, porcupines, lizards, and frogs. Look up and you'll see hawks, owls, woodpeckers, and perhaps a rare (and critically endangered) California condor (pictured here).

TAKE IT EASY

Pack a picnic and spread out a blanket at Vista Encantada off of Cape Royal Road. Soak in stunning views of the surrounding park (above) while you snack.

77

Rock and Roll

1 A visit to the Yavapai Observation Station (below) gets you great views of the canyon, plus a fun lesson in the geology of the area (including a cool carving of the Grand Canyon).

In the Saddle

2 One of the most popular ways to get to the bottom of the canyon is by mule. Opt for a one-day or overnight trip; if you overnight it, you'll cozy up in a cabin in Phantom Ranch at the bottom of the canyon. (Note: For South Rim mule trips, riders must be at least 55 inches [1.4 m] tall. For North Rim trips, they must be at least ten years old.)

Take a Hike

3 Which trails are tops? Try family-friendly Bright Angel Point, Cape Royal, and Cliff Springs Trails—all a mile (1.6 km) long or less and offering sensational views of the canyons. Angling for more adventure? Try the ten-mile (16-km) Widforss Trail for a daylong journey.

Go North

5 The park's less-developed North Rim, 1,000 feet (305 m) higher than the South Rim, is known as "the road less traveled." Here, you'll find quieter trails through a dense forest—and equally amazing sights throughout the summer (heavy snow keeps this area closed from October to mid-May).

[DARE TO EXPLORE]

RIDE THE RAILS
Board the Grand Canyon Railroad—the only train still servicing a national park—and take a trip into the Old West. Performers will keep you entertained on the 2.5-hour ride with songs, skits, and a reenactment of a cowboy shootout.
thetrain.com

HANDS-ON
Feed, pet, and play with deer at the Grand Canyon Deer Farm. You can also see other "residents" like reindeer, wallabies, marmosets, camels, and bison.
deerfarm.com

BRIDGE IN THE SKY
Walk off the edge of a cliff—and onto the Grand Canyon Skywalk, a horseshoe-shaped bridge hanging over the canyon west of the park. Afraid of heights? Don't look down: The bridge, owned by the Hualapai Indian tribe, sits some 4,000 feet (1,219 m) above the Colorado River.
grandcanyonwest.com

AWESOME ERUPTION
Almost 1,000 years ago, a volcano erupted in an area of what is now Flagstaff, Arizona. Today, the scene at Sunset Crater Volcano National Monument remains eerily preserved: A cinder cone rising 1,000 feet (305 m) from the ground surrounded by frozen rivers of lava. About 100 miles (161 km) from the Grand Canyon. **nps.gov/sucr**

Blast From the Past

4 Head to historic Grand Canyon Village, where you'll find buildings dating back to the early 1900s. Stop by the Train Depot and take one of the walking tours. Nearby, you can see the Tusayan Ruin and Museum (left) to get a feel for what life was like for Pueblo Indians 800 years ago.

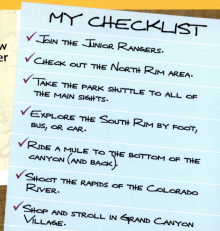

MY CHECKLIST
- ✓ Join the Junior Rangers.
- ✓ Check out the North Rim area.
- ✓ Take the park shuttle to all of the main sights.
- ✓ Explore the South Rim by foot, bus, or car.
- ✓ Ride a mule to the bottom of the canyon (and back).
- ✓ Shoot the rapids of the Colorado River.
- ✓ Shop and stroll in Grand Canyon Village.

FAST FACT: The Grand Canyon is one of the Seven Natural Wonders of the World.

CENTENNIAL EDITION

The National Parks' Other Dimension: Spooky Sites!

TOP: Alcatraz Island
CENTER: Great Sand Dunes National Park
BOTTOM: Death Valley National Park

Not all national parks are about cute animals and rainbows over waterfalls. Some of them have a creepy side. What's spookier than an island prison? How about the devil's golf course? Or a UFO hot spot? Check out these parks if you don't mind your vacation having a side of spooky.

Spooky Factor
Anyone can visit Alcatraz's abandoned cells and listen to recordings of the prison guards and inmates. For maximum spookiness, you can also tour the prison at night.

AL CAPONE

SPOOKY SITE ONE
ALCATRAZ ISLAND, GOLDEN GATE NATIONAL RECREATION AREA
California

Surrounded by San Francisco Bay, Alcatraz Island, aka "The Rock," was once inhabited by notorious criminals, like Chicago mobster Al "Scarface" Capone. Though the prison was considered escape-proof, two inmates once fled on a raft, but were never found. The prison closed in the 1960s.

SPOOKY SITE TWO
DEVILS TOWER NATIONAL MONUMENT
Wyoming

Devils Tower had a starring role in the 1970s alien movie *Close Encounters of the Third Kind*. But the national monument—the nation's first, created in 1906—actually got its name by accident. During a 19th-century expedition to the area, an interpreter mistook the Native American name for the formation as "God's Bad Tower," which later became "Devils Tower." In reality, the name referred to a bear, stemming from Native American legends that the creases in the tower came from a bear clawing at the sides.

SPOOKY SITE THREE
DEATH VALLEY NATIONAL PARK
California

The hottest place on Earth boasts landmarks with names like Hell's Gate, Last Chance Mountain, Devil's Golf Course, and Furnace Creek. With place-names like that, you'd think tourists would go running. But every year, about a million people drop by the park. Most of these places earned their name because Death Valley gets so hot—up to 134°F (57°C) in the summer.

Spooky Factor
Don't bring your clubs to the alien landscape at Devil's Golf Course. The salt pan is covered in rocks that have been formed into jagged spires by rain and wind. As the saying goes, only the devil could play golf on this rough ground.

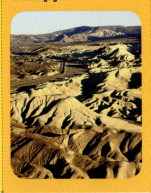

SPOOKY SITE FOUR
GREAT SAND DUNES NATIONAL PARK
Colorado

Sand dunes don't sound so spooky by themselves, but Great Sand Dunes National Park is definitely located in a place of mystery. Summer night programs in the park take advantage of the excellent sky-watching conditions. The best view? The top of the 750-foot (229-m) Star Dune, the tallest dune in the park. Or, you can head outside of the park to the UFO Watchtower, to keep an eye out from the viewing platform.

Spooky Factor
The San Luis Valley, where the park is located, is considered a hotbed of UFO sightings. The woman who runs the UFO Watchtower says some 60 unidentified flying objects have been reported in the area in the last 15 years.

▶ Other Must-see Park Properties in the Southwest

AMISTAD NATIONAL RECREATION AREA (TX)

nps.gov/amis

WHY IT'S COOL: It's an oasis in the desert landscape of southern Texas.

WHAT TO DO: Explore prehistoric rock art and a wide variety of plant and animal life; boating, fishing, swimming, and camping.

TRY THIS: Drive across Amistad Dam for a great view and to check out the Mexico–Texas border.

BANDELIER NATIONAL MONUMENT (NM)

nps.gov/band

WHY IT'S COOL: The area offers a wild landscape and a unique diversity of habitats that are specific to northern New Mexico.

WHAT TO DO: Tour ancestral Puebloan sites; hiking, picnicking, and backpacking.

TRY THIS: Visiting in the winter? Cross-country ski or snowshoe along the Upper Frijoles Trail (also great for hiking in the warmer months).

BIG THICKET NATIONAL PRESERVE (TX)

nps.gov/bith

WHY IT'S COOL: It features an incredible diversity of plants and animals.

WHAT TO DO: Canoeing, rafting, hiking, backpacking, camping, nature walking, and bird-watching.

TRY THIS: Explore the forest by horseback on the Big Sandy Creek Trail.

CANYON DE CHELLY NATIONAL MONUMENT (AZ)

nps.gov/cach

WHY IT'S COOL: It's one of the longest continuously inhabited landscapes of North America; it's also home to a modern community of Navajo people.

WHAT TO DO: Tour the canyon and ruins of ancient dwellings; hiking, camping, and horseback riding.

TRY THIS: Take a scenic drive to several overlooks offering amazing views of the canyon.

CHACO CULTURE NATIONAL HISTORICAL PARK (NM)

nps.gov/chcu

WHY IT'S COOL: It celebrates the culture of an ancient civilization.

WHAT TO DO: Tour cultural sites and ruins; look for petroglyphs; biking, hiking, and camping.

TRY THIS: Hike to Pueblo Bonito in Chaco Canyon, which was constructed in stages between A.D. 850 and 1150 by ancestral Puebloan people.

CHIRICAHUA NATIONAL MONUMENT (AZ)

nps.gov/chir

WHY IT'S COOL: This "Wonderland of Rocks" features stunning rock formations, including pinnacles, columns, spires, and balanced rocks.

WHAT TO DO: Visit Faraway Ranch Historic District, hike, and enjoy scenic drives.

TRY THIS: Up for a challenge? Head to the Heart of Rocks area to see some funky formations like Duck on a Rock, Punch and Judy, and Kissing Rocks.

GILA CLIFF DWELLINGS NATIONAL MONUMENT (NM)

nps.gov/gicl

WHY IT'S COOL: It is home to the stone-and-wood cliff dwellings of the Mogollon people, who lived more than 700 years ago.

WHAT TO DO: Take guided tours of the cliff dwellings, hike the Gila and Aldo Leopold Wilderness areas, camp, and visit nearby hot springs.

TRY THIS: Sign up for an archaeological tour of the TJ Site, an unexcavated pueblo usually closed to the public.

GLEN CANYON NATIONAL RECREATION AREA (AZ, UT)

nps.gov/glca

WHY IT'S COOL: It offers endless water fun on Lake Powell, the second largest man-made reservoir in the United States.

WHAT TO DO: Waterskiing, swimming, boating, fishing, kayaking, hiking, camping, and bicycling.

TRY THIS: Visit Rainbow Bridge, a national monument and the largest known natural rock bridge in the world.

LAKE MEREDITH NATIONAL RECREATION AREA (TX)

nps.gov/lamr

WHY IT'S COOL: The lake offers a refreshing spot in the very hot and dry terrain of the Texas Panhandle.

WHAT TO DO: Boating, waterskiing, sailing, scuba diving, fishing, swimming, camping, horseback riding, and hiking in the backcountry.

TRY THIS: Scale to the top of one of the park's scenic overlooks to catch a stunning sunset.

PADRE ISLAND NATIONAL SEASHORE (TX)

nps.gov/pais

WHY IT'S COOL: It's the longest undeveloped stretch of barrier island in the world.

WHAT TO DO: Beach-combing, windsurfing, fishing, camping, bicycling, wildlife-watching, hiking, and picnicking.

TRY THIS: Attend a public release of sea turtle hatchlings (check in with the visitor center to find out the times).

PETROGLYPH NATIONAL MONUMENT (NM)

nps.gov/petr

WHY IT'S COOL: It's one of the largest petroglyph sites in North America.

WHAT TO DO: Take a hike and check out hundreds of petroglyphs, pictures and designs carved on rocks, that are 400 to 700 years old.

TRY THIS: Use your cellphone wherever you see audio tour signs to listen to park rangers talk about the geology and history of the area.

SANTA FE NATIONAL HISTORIC TRAIL (CO, KS, MO, NM, OK)

nps.gov/safe

WHY IT'S COOL: The trail celebrates the historical significance of this once vital trade route.

WHAT TO DO: Trace the path of the trail using maps and road signs, visit historic sites, and hike trail segments.

TRY THIS: Check out Bent's Old Fort, which served as a supply depot during the Mexican-American War.

Yosemite National Park

Adults can go hang gliding over Yosemite National Park to get a panoramic view of some of the West's most stunning wilderness.

the West

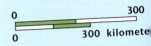

OF ALL OF THE REGIONS in the United States, the West by far has the most national parks. And it's no wonder. Here, you've got it all. You can chill on a tropical island or scale a snow-covered peak. You can hike in the most barren of wildernesses or camp out under a sky sparkling with stars. There are active volcanoes, soaring mountains, majestic glaciers, stunning rock formations, and trees that seem to touch the clouds. Another unique element to the West? The climate is as varied as the landscape: In some locations it's downright cold, like in Mount Rainier in Washington State, while in others it's unbelievably steamy, like in California's Death Valley National Park—the hottest place in the world.

Take a trip to the West and discover large, ancient forests and vast expanses of desert that have been virtually untouched since the days dinosaurs roamed the landscape. Here, you'll find an abundance of animals, from bears to beavers, frogs to foxes, seals to snakes, and almost everything in between. Whatever you do and wherever you roam, one thing's for sure: You will be amazed by the spellbinding sights offered by some of our country's most picturesque parks.

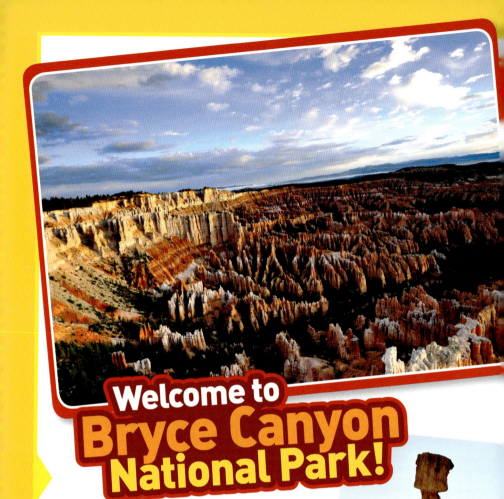

Welcome to Bryce Canyon National Park!

Hoodoo who? In Bryce Canyon National Park, you'll become instantly familiar with this funny word. Hoodoos, or tall and skinny towers of rock sculpted from snowmelt over thousands of years, are the central point of this park. These fascinating stone pillars attract—and mesmerize—the one million visitors who visit Bryce Canyon each year. But this park's not just about funky formations: There are also plenty of trails to tackle, wildlife to watch, and one of the best views of the night sky you'll get from anywhere on Earth.

State: Utah
Established: September 15, 1928
Size: 35,835 acres (14,502 ha)
Website: nps.gov/brca

DISCOVER BRYCE CANYON

RANGER TIPS

The thin air in the park may make you tired, so take breaks as you need them. You should also wear shoes with good soles and ankle support so you don't slip on the rocky trails.

TAKE IT EASY

If you opt to drive to Rainbow Point, stop for a picnic at the end of the route. Relax in the shadows of fir trees while taking in the sights from the park's highest point (9,115 feet [2,778 m]). If you would prefer a simple hike, walk along Queen's Garden Trail (below).

BE EXTREME

Ready to rough it? Set off on the 22.9-mile (36.9-km) Under-the-Rim Trail in Bryce's backcountry. Camp under the stars and see the most remote parts of the park. Note: You must have a permit to hike the backcountry. For a different kind of adventure, visit in the winter (right) and try snowshoeing in the park!

BEST VIEWS

Hit the park early to take in the amazing sunrise at Inspiration Point. The glow from the rising sun paints the hoodoos in hues of red, pink, orange, and yellow. For more stunning views, make sure to visit Bryce Point (above), too!

ALL ABOUT ANIMALS

Keep your eyes open for some of Bryce's 100-plus species of animals, including the endangered Utah prairie dog and the southwestern willow flycatcher. More common creatures? Mule deer (below) and pronghorn.

MY CHECKLIST

✓ Take in the view from Bryce Amphitheater.

✓ Watch the sunrise from Bryce Point.

✓ Get closer to the hoodoos on a walk into a canyon.

✓ Drive to Rainbow Point.

✓ Stay into the evening and stargaze.

✓ Hitch a ride on a horse or mule.

✓ Look out for the endangered Utah prairie dog and other animals.

Camp Out

1 Spend the night under the stars—and under a cover of tall ponderosa pine trees. Choose from two campgrounds within Bryce Canyon National Park. Conveniently, both campgrounds have restrooms, drinking water, and laundry and shower facilities (summer only).

Take a Drive

2 Hop on the free park shuttle and hit all of the key sites and viewpoints (May to October only). Or stay in your car and drive to Rainbow Point, which climbs more than 1,000 feet (305 m)—and along awesome overlooks.

Stargaze

3 At night, Bryce Canyon offers a breathtaking view of the twinkling sky above. Check out some 7,500 stars visible from Bryce during one of the park's regular Night Sky programs.

Take a Hike

4 Explore the park on one of its 12 trails covering 50 miles (80.5 km) and take in the rugged landscape around you. For a great view of the hoodoos hit the 8.6-mile (13.8-km) Peek-a-Boo Trail.

[DARE TO EXPLORE]

COOL CANYON
Check out Red Canyon, home to its own unique red hoodoos, within Dixie National Forest, 9 miles (14.5 km) from Bryce Canyon. **www.fs.usda.gov/dixie**

GO FISH
Head to Fishlake National Forest and cast a line in Fish Lake, hopping with trout, including the hybrid splake and the 35-pound (15.9-kg) Mackinaw. And while you're there, visit the authentic village of the prehistoric Fremont people. About 80 miles (129 km) from Bryce Canyon. **www.fs.usda.gov/fishlake**

RIDE 'EM, COWBOY
See a rodeo at Ruby's Inn, just two minutes from Bryce Canyon's entrance. Every Wednesday to Saturday night, from Memorial Day to mid-August, you can watch bucking broncos and cool cowboys do their thing. **rubysinn.com** (Choose Rodeo under the activities tab.)

HOW GRAND
Hop in the car and head to Grand Staircase–Escalante National Monument, a 30-minute drive from Bryce Canyon. Hike to a cascading waterfall, take in the breathtaking sight of Grosvenor Arch, and explore the land where 75-million-year-old dinosaur fossils have been found.
ut.blm.gov/monument

Get in the Saddle

5 Cruise through the canyons on a guided mule or horseback trek in the park. A two-hour trip tours Bryce Amphitheater and lets you see the park's rock formations up close. (Note: Riders must be at least seven years old.)

FAST FACT: Some hoodoos are taller than a ten-story building!

Welcome to Denali National Park & Preserve!

Spanning an area the size of the state of Massachusetts,

Denali is the home of Mount McKinley, North America's highest peak. And while McKinley (also called Denali) is about as amazing a natural landmark as you can get, it's not all Denali has to offer. Denali is home to a more diverse variety of animals than any other North American park. And when you visit, there's a great chance you'll get to see these amazing creatures, like golden eagles and Dall sheep. But the wildlife that call Denali home are not the only great sights in the park. From its green alpine meadows to its delicate tundra, Denali is packed with scenery unrivaled by any other national park.

State: Alaska
Established: February 26, 1917
Size: 6,075,029 acres (2,458,481 ha)
Website: nps.gov/dena

DISCOVER DENALI

BEST VIEWS

Soak in spectacular views of Mount McKinley (left) at the Eielson Visitor Center. For great views of some of the other mountains in the park, take a hike on the 3-mile (4.8-km) Triple Lakes Trail, where you'll see beautiful views of Mount Fellows, Pyramids Mountain, and other peaks in the Alaska Range.

RANGER TIPS

Denali is a real wilderness, so be sure to read park safety information before you head out. You should also dress for cool, damp weather—even in the summer. When you hit the road, try to go early for better chances to see wildlife (plus you'll beat the crowds!). And there are no refreshments sold in the park, so bring your own snacks and water.

TAKE IT EASY

Venture to Wonder Lake Campground (below) at mile 85 on the Park Road, the closest campground to Mount McKinley. Picnic and chill as the mountain looms large, just 26 miles (41.8 km) away.

BE EXTREME

See Denali from a bird's-eye view on a flight-seeing tour (above). Board a private plane and fly to the tops of the park's peaks, and over its glaciers and lakes.

ALL ABOUT ANIMALS

It would be tough to travel throughout Denali without seeing some of its wildlife. Look for Dall sheep, caribou, moose, wolves, grizzly bears (cub below), black bears, lynx, and more than 160 species of birds, like eagles and falcons.

Take a Tour

4 Join an eco-expert for a lesson about Denali's fields, forests, and mountain trails. Biologists, botanists, artists, and authors all offer hands-on programs throughout the year; ask about them at the visitor center.

Bus It

2 Fill your brain with Denali details by taking a bus tour led by a park naturalist. Trips range from a few hours to all day long and take you deep into the park to give you a chance of seeing big game like moose, grizzly bears, and caribou (left).

Take a Hike

3 Hikes here range from simple strolls to strenuous treks. For a leisurely hike, try the McKinley Station Trail, a 1.5-mile (2.4-km) scenic hike through Denali's dense forest. Another highlight? The Horseshoe Lake Trail, which gives you views of the Nenana River.

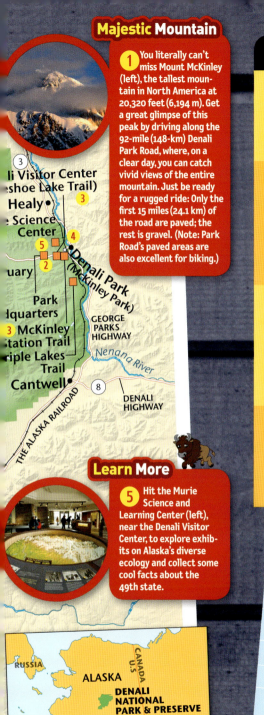

Majestic Mountain

1 You literally can't miss Mount McKinley (left), the tallest mountain in North America at 20,320 feet (6,194 m). Get a great glimpse of this peak by driving along the 92-mile (148-km) Denali Park Road, where, on a clear day, you can catch vivid views of the entire mountain. Just be ready for a rugged ride: Only the first 15 miles (24.1 km) of the road are paved; the rest is gravel. (Note: Park Road's paved areas are also excellent for biking.)

Learn More

5 Hit the Murie Science and Learning Center (left), near the Denali Visitor Center, to explore exhibits on Alaska's diverse ecology and collect some cool facts about the 49th state.

[DARE TO EXPLORE]

ALL ABOARD
See even more of the amazing Alaska wilderness on the Alaska Railroad. Tour guides point out cool sights easily viewed through the train's large windows as you chug past scenic spots. **alaskarailroad.com**

FOR THE DOGS
Meet the amazing huskies that work to patrol the park as part of the Denali ranger team. A tour of the park's kennel offers an inside look at life as a park dog, as rangers share stories about what it's like to "mush." Stop by the visitor center to set up your tour. **nps.gov/dena/planyourvisit/sled-dog-demonstrations.htm**

FASCINATING FOREST
For more stunning glimpses of Alaska's wildlife and wilderness, visit Chugach National Forest in Anchorage (about four hours from Denali). Stroll along some of the forest's 3,550 miles (5,713 km) of coastline, ogle at its glaciers, and spot some of the 200 species of birds that call the Chugach home. **www.fs.usda.gov/chugach/**

MORE MAMMALS
Marvel at moose, mountain goats, and more at Kenai National Wildlife Refuge, in Soldotna, Alaska. Another animal to watch out for? Furry seals lounging around the refuge's two glacier-carved lakes. **www.fws.gov/refuge/kenai/**

MY CHECKLIST
- ✓ Snap some photos of Mount McKinley from various viewpoints.
- ✓ Sign up for a ranger- or naturalist-led program.
- ✓ See the park by bus on a narrated tour.
- ✓ Visit the Murie Science and Learning Center.
- ✓ Drive or bike along Park Road.
- ✓ Go flight-seeing.
- ✓ Bring binoculars and scope out some wildlife from afar!

FAST FACT: Each year, about a thousand climbers attempt to reach Denali's summit. Less than half generally make it to the top.

95

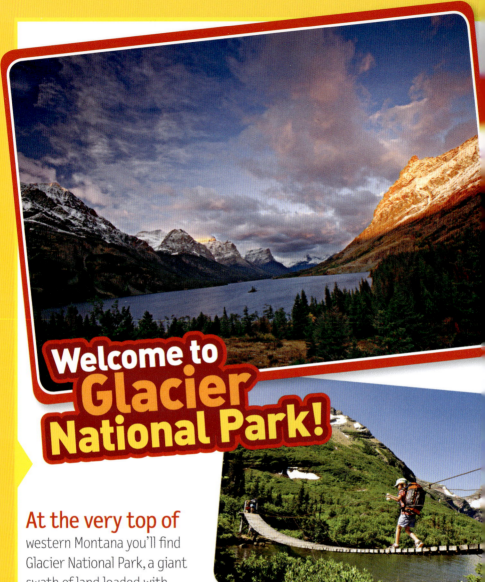

Welcome to Glacier National Park!

At the very top of
western Montana you'll find Glacier National Park, a giant swath of land loaded with majestic mountains, turquoise lakes and streams, lush forests, and an array of animals ranging from bears to bald eagles. This area—commonly referred to as the "crown of the continent"—gets its name from the 15,000-year-old glaciers that once could be found almost everywhere you roamed. Time—and sunshine—have altered that view, and now experts say that in 15 years, there will be no glaciers left in Glacier National Park.

State: Montana
Established: June 18, 1932
Size: 1,013,572 acres (410,179 ha)
Website: nps.gov/glac

96

DISCOVER GLACIER

RANGER TIPS

Glacier is bear country! To stay safe, read all the suggestions for hiking and camping before you visit, and follow them closely. Keep track of where you are in the park by picking up a trail guide at a visitor center.

TAKE IT EASY

There are a number of beautiful lakes in Glacier National Park (above). Hit the beach at Lake McDonald—the largest lake in the park—where you can boat, swim, fish, or hike along the shore. For an easy stroll head to Avalanche Creek for a self-guided walk through the short Trail of the Cedars.

BE EXTREME

For an amazing adventure, go on a multiday white-water-rafting trip on the Middle Fork Flathead River (above). Camping and rafting—what's not to love?

BEST VIEWS

Head to Sun Point via a short nature trail to get a beautiful eyeful of the park's snow-peaked mountains reflecting in the mirror-like surface of St. Mary Lake (below). You can also walk up Avalanche Lake Trail to the glacier-fed Avalanche Lake for wonderful views of the lake, Avalanche Creek, and waterfalls.

ALL ABOUT ANIMALS

Glacier National Park is home to more than 60 species of mammals and more than 260 species of birds (including the beautiful and colorful harlequin duck). There are about 300 grizzly bears in the park—and plenty of black bears, too. But you're more likely to see mountain goats (below), golden-mantled ground squirrels, bighorn sheep, elk, deer, and moose. There are also a number of gray wolf packs that live in parts of the park.

97

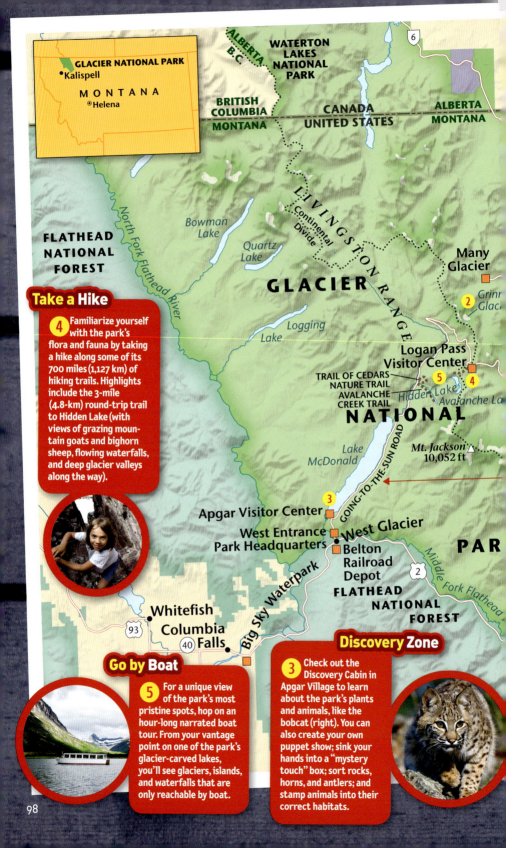

Take a Drive

1 Take a scenic drive along the 50-mile (80.5-km) Going-to-the-Sun Road, which winds through some of the best sights in northwest Montana. Or park your car for the day and use Glacier's free shuttle (left)—you can hop on and off at any or all of the designated shuttle stops.

Take a Tour

2 Learn from an expert! Join ranger-led walks, talks, and amphitheater programs. Up for a trek? Join a naturalist-led hike and boat ride to the edge of Grinnell Glacier. Check at a park visitor center for the most up-to-date list of offerings.

[DARE TO EXPLORE]

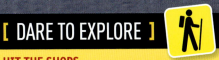

HIT THE SHOPS
Stock up on souvenirs at the Glacier National Park Conservancy gift shop, in the Belton Railroad Depot. Shop for postcards, puzzles, books, games, and more ... whatever you think will preserve memories of your time in Glacier. **glacierconservancy.org**

NATIVE HERITAGE
The town of Browning, Montana—13 miles (20.9 km) from Glacier National Park—is home to about 8,000 of the 13,000 people of the Blackfeet Nation, the largest Native American tribe in Montana. Visit the Blackfeet Reservation and tour the Museum of the Plains Indian or the Blackfeet Heritage Center for authentic artwork and crafts. **blackfeetcountry.com**

SPLASH DOWN
Let loose at the Big Sky Waterpark, about 15 miles (24.1 km) from Glacier. Take a tube down a giant water slide, hurl water balloons at your siblings, and have a blast! **bigskywp.com**

FUN FOREST
More than 2,000 miles (3,219 km) of trails greet you when you reach Flathead National Forest in Kalispell, Montana, about 7 miles (11.3 km) from Glacier. Hiking, boating, climbing, fishing, swimming, and horseback riding are some of the many fun options in this forest.
www.fs.usda.gov/flathead

MY CHECKLIST

✓ Take a drive on Going-to-the-Sun Road.

✓ Ride the park's free shuttle.

✓ Stop by the visitor center to sign up for ranger-led activities.

✓ Check out the Discovery Cabin in Apgar Village.

✓ Chill out at Lake McDonald.

✓ See the sights by boat.

✓ Brave the rapids of the Flathead River.

FAST FACT: Humans first inhabited the Glacier area more than 10,000 years ago.

CENTENNIAL EDITION

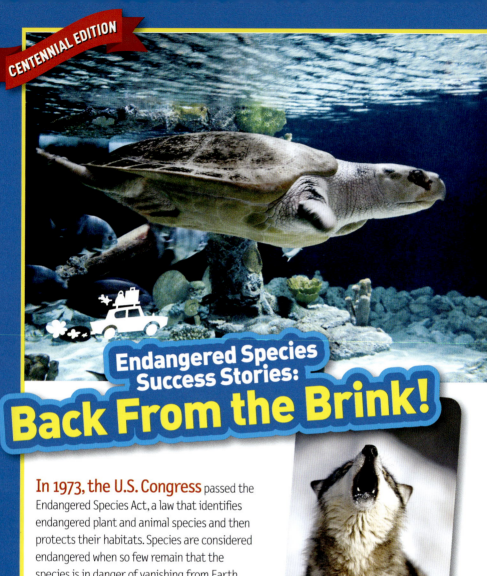

Endangered Species Success Stories:
Back From the Brink!

In 1973, the U.S. Congress passed the Endangered Species Act, a law that identifies endangered plant and animal species and then protects their habitats. Species are considered endangered when so few remain that the species is in danger of vanishing from Earth. Currently, at least one or more endangered species are found in 204 of the more than 400 National Park Service areas. The park service works to reduce the risk of extinction and even restores species that historically lived in the parks but are no longer there because of human disruption. Thanks to the protection given to them in national parks, gray wolves and California condors are making their way back after being on the brink of extinction. The Kemp's Ridley sea turtle still needs help.

TOP: Kemp's Ridley sea turtle
CENTER: Gray wolf
BOTTOM: California condor

SUCCESS STORY ONE
GRAY WOLF

SCIENTIFIC NAME: *Canis lupus*
LOWEST NUMBER RECORDED: A handful in the lower 48 states in the 1930s
NUMBER IN THE WILD NOW: Some 6,000 in the northern Rockies and western Great Lakes
BEST PARKS FOR SPOTTING: Yellowstone, Isle Royale, Voyageurs, Glacier, North Cascades, Grand Tetons, and many Alaska national parks

Gray wolves, once widespread throughout North America, were hunted to near extinction—mostly by settlers in the West who blamed the wolves for killing their livestock. In the 1970s they gained protective status, and in the 1990s they were reintroduced into the greater Yellowstone ecosystem.

HOW TO SPOT A WOLF

Thanks to successful recovery efforts, there are more wolves to see in parks, but they can be tricky to find. The best time to see one is during the wolf's hunting hours—at dawn and dusk. If you're in Yellowstone, Hayden and Lamar Valleys are two of the best spots to see a pack of wolves. You'll need binoculars to get a good look. (Remember it is a park rule that you stay at least 100 yards [91.4 m] away from a gray wolf.) And keep an eye out on the side of the road for clusters of people gathered around telescopes. That's a sure sign there's something exciting to see.

SUCCESS STORY TWO
CALIFORNIA CONDOR

SCIENTIFIC NAME: *Gymnogyps californianus*
LOWEST NUMBER RECORDED: 22 in North America in the 1980s
NUMBER IN THE WILD NOW: 230 living in the wild and another 160 in captivity
BEST PARKS FOR SPOTTING: Grand Canyon National Park, Glen Canyon National Recreation Area, Pinnacles National Park, and Zion National Park

California condors' population plummeted due to lead poisoning caused by eating carcasses containing ammunition fragments or carcasses laced with poison and left out by ranchers to kill coyotes. Today, their numbers have rebounded, and workers catch condors and test their blood to see if there is lead in it. If there is, they treat the bird and release it.

HOW TO SPOT A CALIFORNIA CONDOR

Park rangers know the best ways to spot a California condor. In all the parks that are homes to condors, rangers monitor their whereabouts. California's Pinnacles National Park is home to 27 condors. Hike the trail to High Peaks in the early morning and early evening to watch condors soaring on the thermals. Or head to the campground near the Pinnacles Visitor Center, where telescopes are often set up to give you a better look. Want to see a condor now? Check out this National Park Service link, which has videos of the birds taken by a remote video system: nps.gov/pinn/naturescience/condorvideo.htm

ENDANGERED ALERT
KEMP'S RIDLEY SEA TURTLE

SCIENTIFIC NAME: *Lepidochelys kempii*
NUMBER IN THE WILD NOW: About 1,000 breeding females
BEST PARKS FOR SPOTTING: Padre Island National Seashore

The Kemp's Ridley sea turtle is the most endangered sea turtle. Mainly found in the Gulf of Mexico, their dangerously low numbers are due to overharvesting of their eggs over the last century.

HOW YOU CAN HELP

One of the best things you can do to help the Kemp's Ridley turtle is to protect their nesting sites. If you are in Texas at Padre Island National Seashore between April and mid-July—which is nesting season—and see a sea turtle, sea turtle tracks, or hatchlings, report them to a turtle patroller or park ranger immediately. Biologists will respond to protect the turtles and eggs.

Welcome to Grand Teton National Park!

BISON

The jagged, snow-covered peaks of the Teton Range—the centerpiece of Grand Teton National Park—are a sight you'll simply never get tired of. The range includes its signature peak, Grand Teton, 13,770 feet (4,198 m) and at least 12 pinnacles over 12,000 feet (3,658 m). Occupying a majority of the Jackson Hole valley, the park is not only home to these massive mountains, but also to pristine lakes and rivers, and a wide array of wildlife. In the winter, snow bunnies flock to Grand Teton for top-notch cross-country skiing and snowshoe tours. And in the summer, there's nonstop activity, from hiking to horseback riding.

State: Wyoming
Established: February 26, 1929
Size: 309,994 acres (125,450 ha)
Website: nps.gov/grte

DISCOVER GRAND TETON

RANGER TIPS

Always stand at least 100 yards (91.4 m) away from large animals like bears, bison, moose, and elk. Taking a hike? Bring water, binoculars, camera, sunscreen, and rain gear.

TAKE IT EASY

Head to the swimming beach at Colter Bay and splash around in the cool, clear water or just relax on the rocky shore. There's also an easy three-mile (4.8-km) nature trail here if you get the itch to hit the woods.

BE EXTREME

Get a true bird's-eye view of the Tetons by paragliding (below)! Along with a professional pilot, you will soar high in the sky just outside of the park. No experience necessary, but you have to weigh at least 40 pounds (18 kg) to paraglide. Afraid of heights? Get your thrills on the water with a rafting trip down the Snake River.

BEST VIEW

Check out a vista of the Tetons, Jackson Lake (left), and Snake River from Signal Mountain. For another great view, take a trip on the Jenny Lake Scenic Drive or visit the Snake River Overlook (above).

ALL ABOUT ANIMALS

Look for mule deer, bison, pronghorn, elk, and moose along the trails. On the water? See if you can spot beavers, herons, swans, badgers, and muskrats. If you're lucky, your eyes just may land on a gray wolf, a coyote (cubs below), a mountain lion, and a grizzly or black bear!

Take the Tram

1 The Aerial Tram (below)—mostly used to transport skiers to the summit of the mountain in the winter—is your ticket to the "Top of the Tetons." Year-round, you can hop off the tram and go on a hike or bird-watching expedition or have lunch at a restaurant perched over 4,000 feet (1,219 km) in the sky.

Take a Hike

2 There are more than 200 miles (322 km) of hiking trails winding around the lakes and through the mountains of Grand Teton. Choose from day hikes (like the always popular Cascade Canyon or Granite Canyon Trails) to multiday backpacking trips. Wherever you go, breathtaking scenery and wildlife sightings are guaranteed!

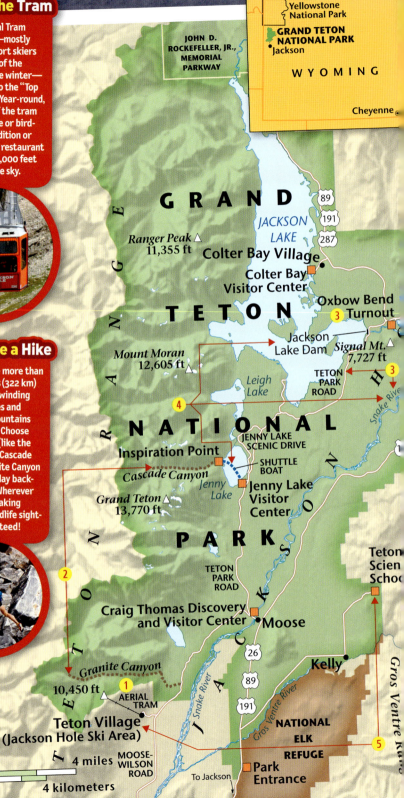

Watch for Wildlife

3 Drive the Teton Park Road with your family and keep your eye out for elk, bison (left), and mule deer on the side of the road. Check out the Snake River area to spot bison, moose, and bald eagles. Oxbow Bend is the place for moose, elk, white pelicans, and river otters.

Hit the Water

4 With dozens of lakes dotting the Teton landscape, there is ample opportunity to explore the park by boat. Hop on the passenger boat across Jenny Lake, or canoe or raft on the Snake River (below) or the Jackson Lake Dam. As you paddle, look for wildlife wallowing at the water's edge.

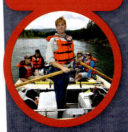

Meet Other Kids

5 From June through September, kids up to ninth grade can hike, play outdoor sports, do science projects (left), and enjoy arts and crafts and water play at Jackson Hole's Kids Ranch in Teton Village. To learn about ecology and the region's natural history, kids can take a summer course taught by the Teton Science School.

[DARE TO EXPLORE]

EYE SOME ELK
About 11,000 elk spread out across the 24,700 acres (9,996 ha) of National Elk Refuge, adjacent to Grand Teton. Visiting in winter? Take a horse-drawn sleigh to see these magnificent animals up close.
fws.gov/refuge/national_elk_refuge

HIT THE TOWN
Spend a day in downtown Jackson, offering family-friendly fun like an alpine slide, mini golf, rodeos, stagecoach rides, souvenir shopping, and more! **jacksonholewy.net**

EXPLORE YELLOWSTONE
The famous geysers and spectacular sights of Yellowstone National Park are just a drive away from Grand Teton. Dedicate a day or two to this just-as-awesome park. **nps.gov/yell**

GET IN THE SADDLE
Experience the Grand Tetons from the back of a horse! Families can choose from one-hour, two-hour, half-day, and full-day rides. Giddy up!
nps.gov/grte/planyourvisit/horserides.htm

MY CHECKLIST
- ✓ Check out the Craig Thomas Discovery & Visitor Center for park info.
- ✓ Look for wildlife along the park's trails, roads, and bodies of water.
- ✓ Join a ranger for a hike, tour, or talk.
- ✓ Ski, snowshoe, or snowboard if visiting in the winter.
- ✓ Take a boat or paddle a canoe along Jenny Lake.
- ✓ Relax and splash at the Colter Bay beach.
- ✓ Don't miss the view from Inspiration Point.

FAST FACT: The 30-pound (13.6-kg) trumpeter swan—the largest bird species in North America—can be found in Grand Teton National Park.

105

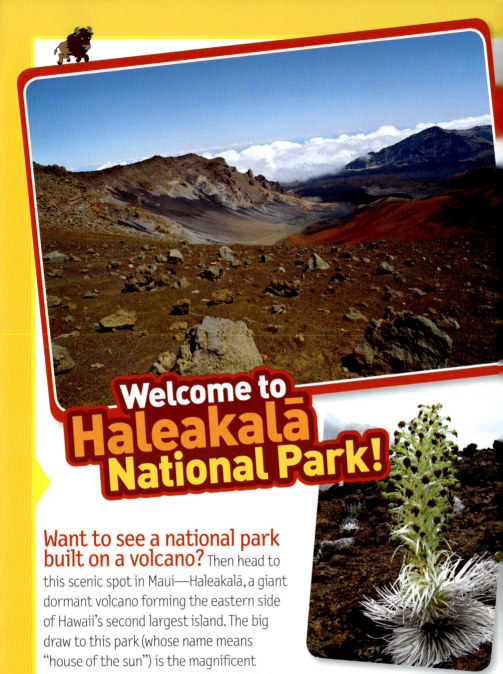

Welcome to Haleakalā National Park!

Want to see a national park built on a volcano?
Then head to this scenic spot in Maui—Haleakalā, a giant dormant volcano forming the eastern side of Hawaii's second largest island. The big draw to this park (whose name means "house of the sun") is the magnificent Haleakalā Crater, stretching seven miles (11.27 km) long and three miles (4.82 km) deep. Hike around the rim of the crater, take a scenic drive through the park, or just gaze into this natural wonder and dream about the days when lava spewed from this massive mountain.

State: Hawaii
Established: August 1, 1916
Size: 34,294 acres (13,878 ha)
Website: nps.gov/hale

106

DISCOVER HALEAKALĀ

BEST VIEW

The view at the Puʻu ʻUlaʻula Summit is just as memorable as the name (which means "red hill"). At an elevation of more than 10,000 feet (3,048 m), you can see the giant volcanoes on the Big Island, plus the neighboring islands of Lanai and Molokai. Sometimes, at night, you can even see the city lights of the island of Oahu to the northwest.

RANGER TIPS

Take two days to explore the park: one on the Haleakalā summit (above) and the other in the Kipahulu coastal regions. The summit is windy, damp, and about 30 degrees (17 Celsius degrees) cooler than the coast, so make sure to pack a jacket! You should also bring your own food and water; neither is sold in Haleakalā National Park.

TAKE IT EASY

Take a relaxing—and refreshing—dip in the cool pools and waterfalls below the highway bridge in ʻOheʻo Gulch (right). Note: This area can be crowded, so keep traveling upstream for a quieter swimming spot. Looking for a great picnic area? Head to Hosmer Grove, located above the park entrance. Beautiful pine and eucalyptus trees surround this shady, cool spot.

BE EXTREME

Take a walk on the wet side with a park naturalist through the Waikamoi Preserve. Be prepared to get muddy as you wind your way 600 feet (183 m) up a Hawaiian forest (left) on this five-mile (8-km), five-hour tour.

ALL ABOUT ANIMALS

Haleakalā is one of the very few last sanctuaries for the honeycreeper (below), a tiny, rare native Hawaiian bird. You'll also spot Maui parrotbills, Hawaiian geese, and sea turtles in this environmentally diverse park.

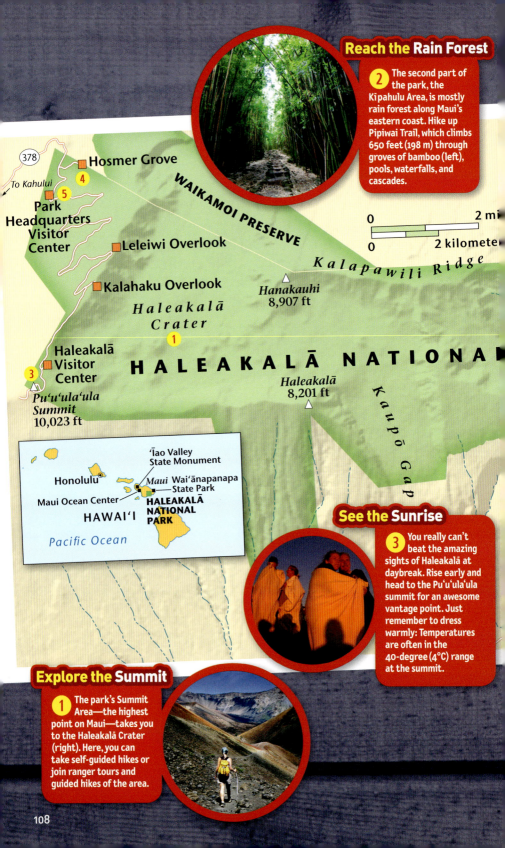

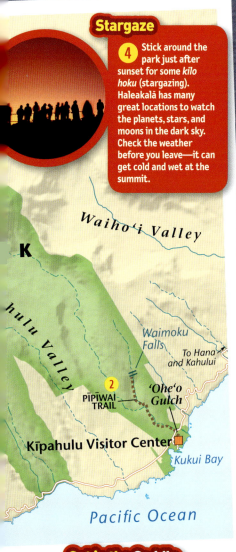

Stargaze

4 Stick around the park just after sunset for some *kilo hoku* (stargazing). Haleakalā has many great locations to watch the planets, stars, and moons in the dark sky. Check the weather before you leave—it can get cold and wet at the summit.

Get in the Saddle

5 Private tour groups offer guided horseback rides in Haleakalā. Hop in the saddle and enjoy breathtaking sights as you wend through this lush tropical wilderness. Make a trip to the visitor center to find out more about the tours.

[DARE TO EXPLORE]

WAI'ĀNAPANAPA NOT?
Explore a cave, fish in the surf, and stroll along the ancient coastal trail in Wai'ānapanapa State Park. About 80 miles (129 km) from Haleakalā National Park. **dlnr.hawaii.gov/dsp/parks/maui/waianapanapa-state-park**

JUNGLE FUN
Get lost in the lush Iao Valley State Monument, featuring a natural rock pinnacle rising 1,200 feet (366 m) into the sky. Walk around a botanic garden and splash around in shallow streams and lagoons. About 40 miles (64.4 km) from Haleakalā National Park. **dlnr.hawaii.gov/dsp/parks/maui**

FISH FRENZY
Hit the Maui Ocean Center and check out hammerhead sharks, eels, octopi, jellyfish, seahorses, Hawaiian green sea turtles, and a 54-foot (16.5-m)-long clear tunnel traveling through a tank of more than 2,000 fish. **mauioceancenter.com**

GO DEEP
Board a submarine and sink more than 100 feet (30.5 m) below the ocean's surface, where you'll see natural coral reefs, fish, marine life—and a replica of a 19th-century ship creating an awesome artificial reef. **atlantisadventures.com**

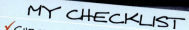

MY CHECKLIST
- ✓ Check out the Haleakalā Crater.
- ✓ Roam through the rain forest valley of Kīpahulu.
- ✓ Hike up to a waterfall.
- ✓ Go swimming in the cool pools.
- ✓ Catch a rare glimpse of a honeycreeper bird.
- ✓ See the sunrise from the summit.
- ✓ Stay into the evening and stargaze.

FAST FACT: You pass through as many ecological zones on a two-hour drive to the summit of Haleakalā as you would on a journey from Mexico to Canada.

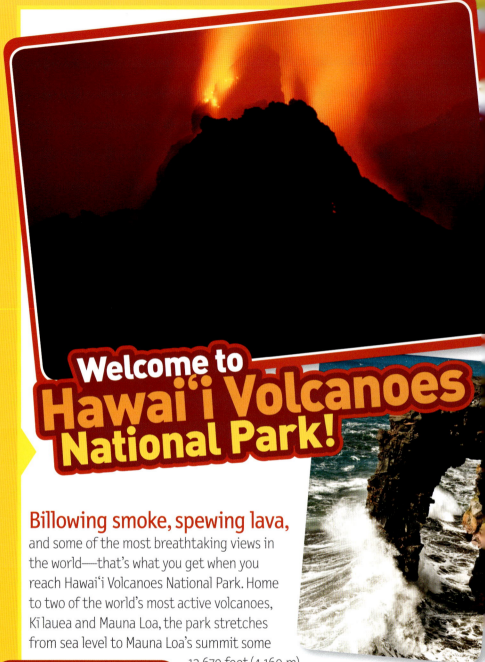

Welcome to Hawai'i Volcanoes National Park!

Billowing smoke, spewing lava, and some of the most breathtaking views in the world—that's what you get when you reach Hawai'i Volcanoes National Park. Home to two of the world's most active volcanoes, Kīlauea and Mauna Loa, the park stretches from sea level to Mauna Loa's summit some 13,679 feet (4,169 m) above the sea. From the eerie, rugged lava trails of Mauna Loa's wilderness area to the lush, green slopes of Kīlauea, the park is distinguished by its diverse landscape, which makes it a must-see spot on Hawaii's Big Island.

State: Hawaii
Established: August 1, 1916
Size: 333,000 acres (134,761 ha)
Website: nps.gov/havo

DISCOVER HAWAI'I VOLCANOES

RANGER TIPS

Active volcanoes can be dangerous. Be sure to read the signage carefully. It's also important to stay on marked trails and off of cliffs or steam vents, which can be unstable and slippery.

TAKE IT EASY

Take a breather on the observation deck at the Thomas A. Jaggar Museum. Clear your mind and just take in nature's beauty as you look at the eruptive activity at Halema'uma'u Crater (below).

BEST VIEW

Head to the Halema'uma'u Overlook, about a ten-minute walk from the Jaggar Museum, for an awesome look into Halema'uma'u Crater (left), which is known as the home of Madame Pele, goddess of Hawaiian volcanoes. The crater is about 3,000 feet (914 m) across and almost 300 feet (91.4 m) deep.

ALL ABOUT ANIMALS

Hawai'i Volcanoes is home to critters of all shapes and sizes. Keep your eyes peeled for carnivorous caterpillars, honeycreepers, turtles, hawks, bats, geese, the giant Hawaiian dragonfly (a unique insect with a five-inch [12.7-cm] wingspan, making it one of the largest dragonflies in the United States), and the happy face spider (pictured here).

BE EXTREME

Cycle down a volcano! Private tour companies will take you on a downhill adventure from the summit of Kīlauea Volcano to the sea (left). On your way down, you'll get to see the volcano up close and personal as you ride through the rain forest and over lava flows. Ask about bike tours at the visitor center.

Cool Tube

3 Take a walk through the Thurston Lava Tube (aka Nahuku, right), formed hundreds of years ago when scalding lava seared a tunnel through a rock. Reach it by taking an easy 15-minute-loop trail.

Take a Hike

1 Explore the park on foot! There are plenty of trails through rain forests, deserts, and lava flows. One fun destination? The petroglyphs (below) at Pu'u Loa, a sacred place to the people of Hawaii.

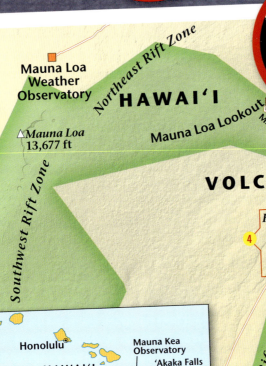

Learn More

2 Stop by the Thomas A. Jaggar Museum to check out exhibits on volcanoes (including a real seismograph and lava rocks you can touch, left), talk to park rangers, and get a great view of the Kīlauea Caldera and the steaming Halema'uma'u.

112

Take a Drive

4 Soak in stunning views from your car by traveling two roads that wind through the park. The 11-mile (17.7-km) Crater Rim Drive, which includes overlooks (below), loops around Kīlauea Summit and through the lush rain forest; the Chain of Craters Road leads to lava flows and awesome views of impressive craters.

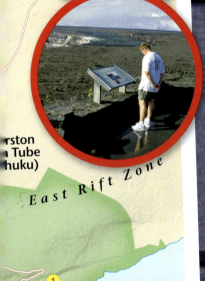

East Rift Zone

1 Pu'u Loa Petroglyphs

Stay Late

5 After you spend the day exploring, stick around for After Dark in the Park. This program—usually held every Tuesday at 7 p.m. at the Kīlauea Visitor Center Auditorium—features everything from experts speaking about unique elements of the park to live music and entertainment.

[DARE TO EXPLORE]

STAR POWER
Love to stargaze? Head to Mauna Kea, the world's highest island mountain and home of the Mauna Kea Observatory. View the night sky from one of the telescopes, including one that is 16 inches (40.6 cm) wide! ifa.hawaii.edu/info/vis

SEE THE FALLS
Head to 'Akaka Falls State Park to take a walk on a paved path and catch amazing views of the 100-foot (30.5-m) cascading Kahuna Falls. About 15 miles (24.1 km) from the park. dlnr.hawaii.gov/dsp/parks/hawaii/akaka-falls-state-park

FIN FUN
Get in the swim of things by diving into Dolphin Quest, home to a friendly bunch of Atlantic bottlenose dolphins. Pet them, feed them, and watch them flip and leap all around you. In Waikoloa, about 70 miles (113 km) from the park. dolphinquest.com

BLACK BEACH
Get a chance to stroll down the newest beach in the world! Kaimu Black Sand Beach in Pahoa dates only to March 2008. Wiggle your toes in the jet-black sand (formed from ground lava rock) as lava flows off Kīlauea in the distance. Across the road from the Kalapana Village Café, about 20 miles (32.2 km) from the park.

MY CHECKLIST
- ✓ Soak in summit views by car or by foot.
- ✓ Walk through the Thurston Lava Tube.
- ✓ Peek at the petroglyphs at Pu'u Loa.
- ✓ Check out the exhibits at the Thomas A. Jaggar Museum.
- ✓ Ride a bike down the volcano.
- ✓ Look for lava flows and steam vents.
- ✓ Join a ranger-led program to find out more about the park.

FAST FACT: Since it began erupting in 1983, Kīlauea has spewed enough lava to make a pathway to the moon and back five times!

113

Welcome to Joshua Tree National Park!

Joshua Tree may be smack in the middle of a dry desert, but that doesn't mean it's void of living things. The Joshua tree forest in this park is the largest, tallest, and densest Joshua Tree Forest in the United States. And this national park is packed with other plants, too. Colorful ocotillos and desert grasses and wildflowers make this a unique landscape. There are also many animals that call Joshua Tree home (jackrabbits, bighorn sheep, iguanas, and quail are just some of the creatures that may catch your eye). Another fun feature of Joshua Tree? Some of the funkiest rock formations you'll see in North America, plus massive boulders, just perfect for climbing on!

State: California
Established: October 31, 1994
Size: 794,000 acres (321,321 ha)
Website: nps.gov/jotr

DISCOVER JOSHUA TREE

RANGER TIPS

When climbing on the rocks, watch where you put your hands; there are rattlesnakes in Joshua Tree. There are also old mine shafts along some of the hiking trails. Never enter one of these mines—it is unsafe and prohibited.

TAKE IT EASY

Kick back and relax in Cottonwood Spring, a cool, palm-shaded oasis near the southern park entrance. While you relax, make sure to look up. This oasis provides shelter for many bird species, like the rock wren (right).

BE EXTREME

Go rock climbing (below)! Joshua Tree features more than 400 climbing formations and 8,000 climbing routes. Link up with a guide for important instruction and equipment, then get ready to (literally) scale new heights!

BEST VIEW

Take the six-mile (9.7-km) trip to Keys View, where you'll score a panoramic view of the Coachella Valley (above), the Salton Sea, and the Sonoran Desert mountains in Mexico. Across the valley you'll see 10,800-foot (3,292-m) San Jacinto Peak standing tall over Palm Springs.

ALL ABOUT ANIMALS

Typical wildlife includes birds (look for roadrunners, mockingbirds, and quail), lizards (like the Chuckwalla, below), toads, and ground squirrels—though you may also spot snakes, bighorn sheep, coyotes, and black-tailed jackrabbits.

See the "Trees"

1 You can't miss the park's namesake plant, the Joshua tree (right). Learn more about the iconic plant and the rest of the region's diverse desert ecology through displays at the Oasis Visitor Center.

Take a Tour

2 Sign up for a guided tour of the Keys Ranch (below), located in a remote, rocky canyon. Go back in time and glimpse what it took to live and thrive in the Mojave Desert more than 100 years ago.

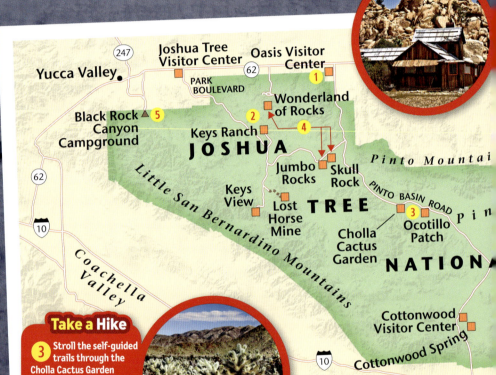

Take a Hike

3 Stroll the self-guided trails through the Cholla Cactus Garden (right) and the Ocotillo Patch, where you can see the Colorado Desert ecosystem up close.

Rock Stars

4 Make a point to check out Joshua Tree's collection of supercool rock formations that happen to look a lot like humans, dinosaurs, monsters, cathedrals, or castles. Look for Jumbo Rocks, Skull Rock (left), and the Wonderland of Rocks.

Camp Out

5 Pitch a tent at the mouth of a canyon at the quiet, family campground at Black Rock Canyon. Sleep under the stars while surrounded by Joshua trees, junipers, cholla cacti, and a variety of desert shrubs.

[DARE TO EXPLORE]

GIANT ROCK
Check out Giant Rock, located just north of Joshua Tree National Park in Landers. At seven stories high and weighing more than 23,000 tons (20,865 MT), it's considered the world's largest freestanding boulder.
lucernevalley.net/giantrock

SADDLE UP
Explore the mountainous desert terrain around Joshua Tree by horseback on a guided tour. You'll travel along equestrian trails and see open lands, canyon bottoms, and dry washes. One- or two-hour rides are available. **crazyhorseranch.biz**

MORE MOJAVE
Giant sand dunes, volcanic cinder cones, Joshua tree forests, and beautiful wildflowers are all found at the 1.6-million-acre (647,497-ha) Mojave National Preserve, about a two-hour drive from Joshua Tree. Hint: Run down the "singing" sand dunes to make them go boom! **nps.gov/moja**

EXPLORE THE PRESERVE
Watch whiptail lizards dash across the ground and scramble over rocks at Indian Canyons, a preserve that belongs to the Agua Caliente band of Cahuilla Indians. Hike up Murray Canyon, and don't forget your bathing suit—there's a pristine pool under a waterfall for you to cool off in after your climb. About 40 miles (64.4 km) from Joshua Tree. **indian-canyons.com**

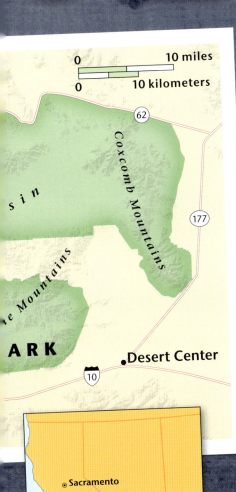

MY CHECKLIST
- ✓ Start at a visitor center for up-to-the-minute park info.
- ✓ Meander along a nature trail.
- ✓ Check out the vistas from Keys View.
- ✓ Join a guided walking tour of Keys Ranch.
- ✓ Get active! Mountain climb or bike around the park.
- ✓ Camp out by a canyon.
- ✓ See the park's funky rock formations and old mines.

FAST FACT: Joshua trees only grow in the Mojave Desert.

Welcome to Mount Rainier National Park!

Welcoming up to two million visitors a year, Mount Rainier is one of the most ecologically diverse national parks in the nation. There are five developed areas in Mount Rainier: Longmire, Paradise, Ohanapecosh, Sunrise, and Carbon/Mowich. At the center of it all? Mount Rainier, an active volcano that last erupted over a century ago. Surrounding this enormous peak is a magnificent wilderness where you can stroll through blankets of wildflowers, listen for cracking glacier debris, wander through trees more than a thousand years old, and play in the snow all winter long.

State: Washington
Established: March 2, 1899
Size: 236,381 acres (95,660 ha)
Website: nps.gov/mora

DISCOVER MOUNT RAINIER

RANGER TIPS

Mount Rainier is an active volcano! Make sure you check conditions of the mountain before heading out on a hike. And dress for the mountain's unstable weather by carrying extra clothes and rain gear.

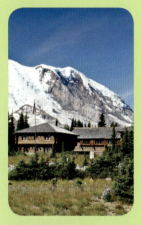

TAKE IT EASY

Travel 2,500 feet (762 m) in ten minutes on the Mount Rainier Gondola (top) to the summit of Crystal Mountain. There, you can eat at the Summit House, the highest restaurant in Washington State.

BE EXTREME

Rent a bike (below) and hit the park's pipeline trail. Follow this mostly flat, dirt road until you hit Packwood Lake, where you can soak up the views of Rainier and the Goat Rocks Wilderness. If you're in the mood for an exciting hike, head to the Carbon River at the park's northwest corner entrance. Here you can check out a rain forest and hike to a dark, shiny glacier. Note: Check for road closures before you head out.

BEST VIEW

Head to the Sunrise Visitor Center (left) for some of the most amazing sights in the park. From 6,400 feet (1,951 m) above sea level, you'll take in views of Mount Rainier, Emmons Glacier, and other volcanoes in the Cascade Range.

ALL ABOUT ANIMALS

The diverse landscape of Mount Rainier provides habitats for all kinds of animals, such as elk, deer, goats, black bears, marmots, birds (like the Clark's nutcracker, below), fish, and frogs. Invertebrates are the most abundant, making up 85 percent of all animals in the park.

119

Take a Hike

1 The park has huge hike potential—260 miles (418 km) of maintained trails, to be exact. Check out the Nisqually Vista Trail, a 1.2-mile (1.9-km) loop trail with great views of Mount Rainier. Or head to the Sunrise Visitor Center to find trailheads for hikes like the Sourdough Ridge Trail, offering sights of Mount Rainier, glaciers, and other volcanoes in the Cascade Range.

Great Glacier

4 Head to Nisqually Glacier (below), the best known of the park's 25 glaciers. Get there by walking about a mile (1.6 km) from the Glacier View Overlook (on the road that leads from Nisqually to Paradise).

Snow Cool

5 Visiting in the winter? Hit the Paradise area for all sorts of "cool" fun. Park rangers lead guided snowshoe walks on weekends from late December through early April (leaving from the Henry M. Jackson Memorial Visitor Center at Paradise). You can also go snowboarding, skiing, and tubing when there's sufficient snow.

[DARE TO EXPLORE]

GO TO GIFFORD
Snag spectacular views of Mount St. Helens from Gifford Pinchot National Forest, about 10 miles (16.1 km) from Mount Rainier National Park. You can also see glaciers and a variety of plants and animals spread across seven wilderness areas.
www.fs.usda.gov/giffordpinchot

RAD REGROWTH
The 1980 eruption of Mount St. Helens destroyed every living thing around it. Today, a beautiful forest has emerged from the once charred land, which you can explore at Mount St. Helens National Volcanic Monument, located within Gifford Pinchot National Forest.
www.fs.usda.gov/mountsthelens

ALL ABOARD
Take a scenic ride through the countryside aboard the Mount Rainier Scenic Railroad, a vintage logging locomotive. Listen as the conductor offers a history lesson of the breathtaking sights you pass on the two-hour journey. **mrsr.com**

WILDLIFE GALORE
You're guaranteed to see some cool animals at the Northwest Trek Wildlife Park near Eatonville, Washington (about 25 miles [40.2 km] from the park). Search for wildlife like bears, bison, wolves, owls, and more as you wander through forests, wetlands, and meadows on the park's tram.
nwtrek.org

MY CHECKLIST
- ✓ Take a glimpse at a glacier.
- ✓ Walk to a waterfall.
- ✓ Hit the trails or take in a nature walk.
- ✓ Ride the gondola to the summit of Crystal Mountain.
- ✓ Play in Paradise's snow park during the winter.
- ✓ Earn a Junior Ranger badge.
- ✓ Ride a bike along the park's pipeline trail.

FAST FACT: There are 25 glaciers, 392 lakes, and 470 rivers and streams in Mount Rainier.

CENTENNIAL EDITION

Get the Scoop on Finding Fossils:
Dig In!

If you dig ancient history, then the national parks have some perfectly petrified places to see fossils. Remember that these ancient treasures should stay in parks for all to enjoy. Do not remove any bits of nature—no matter how small—from a park. Instead, take a photo, make a sketch, or write about your awesome find.

TOP: Petrified Forest National Park
CENTER: Dinosaur National Monument
BOTTOM: Fossil Butte National Monument

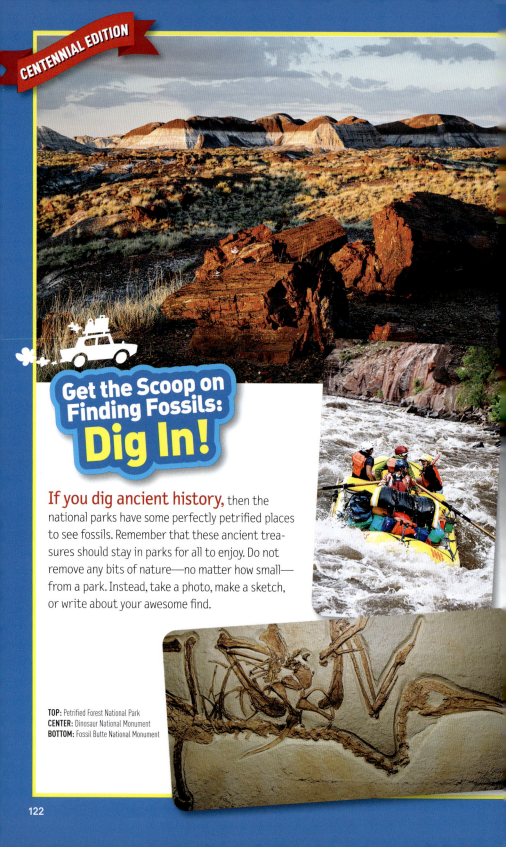

STOP ONE
DINOSAUR NATIONAL MONUMENT
Colorado & Utah

Discover a land that dinosaurs once roamed. Dinosaur National Monument, located in Colorado and Utah, is home to literally tons of skeletons and skulls from the Jurassic period, 205–138 million years ago. Fifteen hundred bones of dinosaurs are encased in rock at Dinosaur Quarry Exhibit Hall, including *Allosaurus, Stegosaurus, Diplodocus,* and *Apatosaurus*. (The Utah side of the park is the one where dinosaur fossils have been found.) Take a 1.5-hour ranger-led "fossil discovery" trail hike, leaving daily from Quarry Exhibit Hall, and learn about fossils, as well as the park's evidence of their ancient ecosystems. When you're ready to cool off, try rafting the park's Green and Yampa Rivers. Float down channels surrounded by towering cliffs.

Dinosaur National Monument was the **FIRST PLACE TO LEAVE FOSSILS** where they were found for public viewing, rather than excavating them.

STOP TWO
FOSSIL BUTTE NATIONAL MONUMENT
Wyoming

Dinosaurs aren't the only fossils worth checking out. At Fossil Butte National Monument, in southwestern Wyoming, you can see fossilized fish, insects, birds, reptiles, and mammals from up to 56 million years ago. Fine-grained sediment and still water preserved these skeletons, which have provided scientists with research fodder ever since. The fossils were discovered by coal miners more than 100 years ago. Check out the park's visitor center to see more than 300 fossils, including a 13-foot (4-m)-long crocodile. In the summer, you may be able to hike out to the fossil research quarry and catch a glimpse of a scientist studying a new discovery. Check the park's schedule for observation hours.

Railroad workers in the 1860s were some of the **FIRST PEOPLE TO UNCOVER** major fossil finds in the Fossil Butte area.

STOP THREE
PETRIFIED FOREST NATIONAL PARK
Arizona

What happens to wood after 200 million years? Under the right conditions, it becomes petrified! During the Triassic period, 248–205 million years ago, logs now found in and around Arizona's Petrified Forest National Park were buried in a river by sediment and debris. Oxygen was cut off from the wood, which dramatically slowed the decaying process. Then, minerals from volcanic ash were absorbed into the wood over thousands of years and crystallized in the wood's cells, eventually replacing the organic material that was once there. If a log was cracked or crushed, clear quartz, purple amethyst, and smoky quartz formed over time in the void. Starting around 60 million years ago, the buried petrified wood was unearthed during the uplifting of the Colorado Plateau. The petrified wood you see at the park is hard and brittle. And wood isn't the only thing that can be petrified. Leaves, pollen, and spores can, too! Stop in at the park's Painted Desert visitor center to learn more about the park's geology, and take a hike around the park's seven trails to check out the petrified wood in person.

Petrified wood **WEIGHS ABOUT 168 POUNDS** per cubic foot (2,691 kg/m^3)!

123

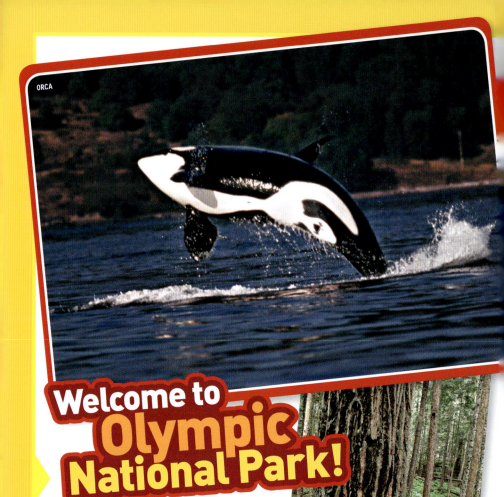

ORCA

Welcome to Olympic National Park!

Warmly referred to as "a gift from the sea,"

Olympic National Park preserves 73 miles (117 km) of Washington State coastal wilderness. The park features three major ecosystems (subalpine, coastal, and forest), which include emerald green rain forests, rocky strips of coastline, natural hot springs, more than 3,000 miles (4,828 km) of rivers and streams, and some of the world's oldest trees. Olympic is also home to many different animals, including 37 species of native fish. It's no wonder that more than three million people visit this spot every year, making it one of the country's most popular national parks.

State: Washington
Established: June 29, 1938
Size: 922,000 acres (373,121 ha)
Website: nps.gov/olym

DISCOVER OLYMPIC

RANGER TIPS

This park is huge! Ask a ranger for recommendations on things to do based on how much time you have to explore the park. When traveling along the coast, know the tides; bring a map and tide chart to plan your route. And make sure to bring rain gear and layer up—weather around Olympic is unpredictable.

BEST VIEW

Climb to Hurricane Ridge (above), where you'll see the awesome Olympic Mountains (even more amazing at sunset). While you're up there, look for the Olympic marmot!

ALL ABOUT ANIMALS

Elk, elk, and more elk (below)! Olympic is home to the largest unmanaged herd of Roosevelt elk in the world. You may also see mountain goats, pikas, squirrels, lynx, foxes, coyotes, wolverines, grizzly bears, bighorn sheep, and about 300 species of birds. On the water? Watch for dolphins, whales, sea lions, seals, and sea otters. Just remember to watch all wildlife from a distance.

TAKE IT EASY

Chill out at Rialto Beach (above). Collect driftwood on its rocky shores, climb on giant logs, and take in views of the park's iconic seastacks (rock formations in the water). If you're up for a short hike, walk 1.5 miles (2.4 km) north to see Hole-in-the-Wall, a stunning sea-carved arch.

BE EXTREME

Ride the rapids (below)! A guide will take you on an exciting course down the Elwha River, the Hoh River, or straight through the heart of the Hoh Rain Forest. Whatever water you hit, get ready for a *splash*-tastic time! If you're visiting in the winter, go sledding at Hurricane Ridge. Note: Check weather conditions and park closure information before you go.

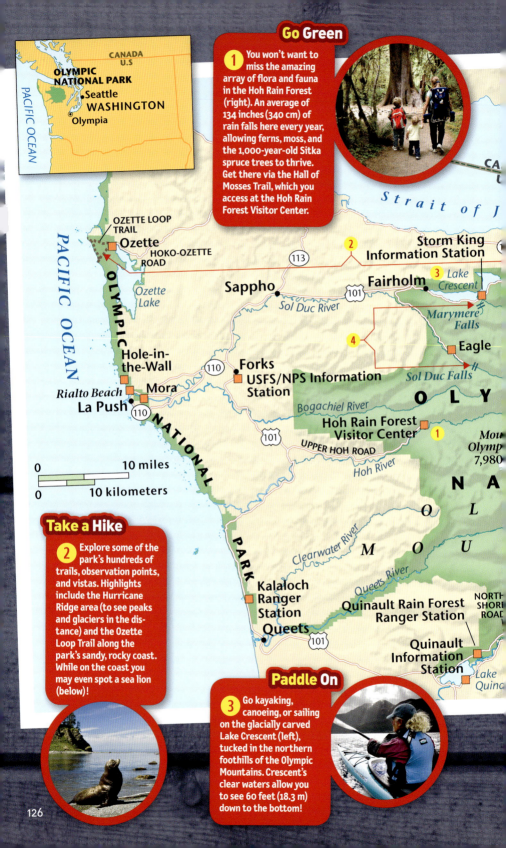

Go Green

1 You won't want to miss the amazing array of flora and fauna in the Hoh Rain Forest (right). An average of 134 inches (340 cm) of rain falls here every year, allowing ferns, moss, and the 1,000-year-old Sitka spruce trees to thrive. Get there via the Hall of Mosses Trail, which you access at the Hoh Rain Forest Visitor Center.

Take a Hike

2 Explore some of the park's hundreds of trails, observation points, and vistas. Highlights include the Hurricane Ridge area (to see peaks and glaciers in the distance) and the Ozette Loop Trail along the park's sandy, rocky coast. While on the coast you may even spot a sea lion (below)!

Paddle On

3 Go kayaking, canoeing, or sailing on the glacially carved Lake Crescent (left), tucked in the northern foothills of the Olympic Mountains. Crescent's clear waters allow you to see 60 feet (18.3 m) down to the bottom!

126

Follow the Falls

4 Take a 0.8-mile (1.3-km) hike to Sol Duc Falls (left), a trio of falls crashing down to a black rock crevasse below. Or, from Lake Crescent, take a quick hike to the 90-foot (27.4-m)-high Marymere Falls.

[DARE TO EXPLORE]

DISCOVER MORE
Visit the Olympic Coast Discovery Center to learn more about marine wildlife in the area. It's also a great spot to search for whales out in the water. **olympiccoast.noaa.gov/about/welcome.html**

GO ON SAFARI
Take a safari through Olympic's Quinault Rain Forest. From the comforts of a bus, you can see huge (and ancient!) trees and wildlife, and learn fun facts provided by knowledgeable guides. **beelinetours.com/rainforest-safaris**

TWILIGHT TOUR
"Twihards" flock to Forks, the town featured in the Twilight book series by Stephenie Meyer. Pick up a packet at the Forks Chamber of Commerce visitor center for a map that will take you to some of the most memorable sites from the books. About 100 miles (161 km) from Olympic National Park. **forkswa.com**

AMAZING ANIMALS
Get up close and personal with wildlife at the Olympic Game Farm, originally a home for animal actors featured in Disney movies back in the 1960s. Today, the farm is open to the public and features a bevy of animals, from lions to llamas. **olygamefarm.com**

MY CHECKLIST
- ✓ Visit the Hoh Rain Forest.
- ✓ Hike to Hurricane Ridge.
- ✓ Ride the rapids of the Elwha or Hoh rivers.
- ✓ Stroll the rocky coast and see a seastack.
- ✓ Gawk at must-see trees, like the Sitka spruce.
- ✓ Paddle along Lake Crescent.
- ✓ Have more fun at the Children's Discovery Center!

Discover More

5 Dress up like a park ranger, play games, and get hands-on with artifacts like deer antlers and animal fur at the Children's Discovery Room at the Olympic National Park Visitor Center.

FAST FACT: Winds at Hurricane Ridge can blow up to 75 miles an hour (121 km/h)!

Welcome to Rocky Mountain National Park!

Lift your senses to a new level in

Rocky Mountain National Park. With elevations ranging from 8,000 feet (2,438 m) to 14,259 feet (4,346 m), you'll see all sorts of amazing sights, from jagged snowcapped mountains to colorful blooms of wildflowers to pristine lakes. Just under 80 miles (129 km) from Denver, this park features 359 miles (578 km) of hiking trails, each offering an amazing, up-close-and-personal peek at wetlands, forests, and tundra. Whether you visit in the winter, spring, summer, or fall, you're bound to be wowed by the Rockies.

State: Colorado
Established: January 26, 1915
Size: 265,873 acres (107,595 ha)
Website: nps.gov/romo

DISCOVER ROCKY MOUNTAINS

RANGER TIPS

Take your time and drink plenty of water. The Rockies' thin air may tire you out and dehydrate you more quickly than normal. You should also layer up! The weather in the Rockies shifts drastically during the day, so be prepared for both hot and cold temperatures. And be aware of your surroundings: Mountain lion and black bear sightings have increased over the past several years.

BEST VIEW

Head to the Alpine Visitor Center, located 11,798 feet (3,596 m) above sea level, for unrivaled glimpses at ancient glacial valleys, alpine tundra (right), and Fall River. You can also head to Sprague Lake to take an easy half-mile (0.8-m) nature walk where you will be surrounded by amazing views of the magical mountain peaks of the Continental Divide.

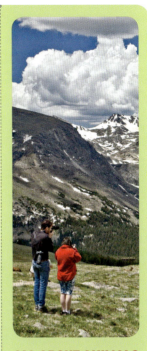

TAKE IT EASY

Go for a picnic! The park has many opportunities for picnicking, both on the east side and the west side of the park. Popular spots are Sprague Lake on the east and Coyote Valley on the west. Dream Lake (above) is also a great place to fish and enjoy the view.

BE EXTREME

Take a rock-climbing course (right) with the Colorado Mountain School, an organization authorized to teach kids how to climb in the park.

ALL ABOUT ANIMALS

The park is famous for its large animals, like elk, bighorn sheep (below), moose, and mule deer. You may also see coyotes, black bears, cougars, and hundreds of smaller animals. Beautiful butterflies are also found all over the area (there are 141 species in the park!).

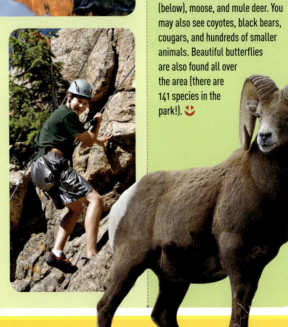

Take a Hike

2 Explore Rocky Mountains by hiking one of its many trails. One family favorite? The Bear Lake Trail, an easy one-mile (1.6-km) round-trip hike that's ripe with wildflowers in the summer and features the stunning sight of Hallett and Longs Peaks reflected in the lake's mirrorlike waters.

Take a Drive

1 Go for a scenic journey along Trail Ridge Road (below), the highest continuous highway in the United States. Look out your window and watch landscapes like mountains, valleys, and tundra pass you by.

Snow Fun

3 Hitting the park in the winter? Go snowshoeing or sledding! (Just make sure your parents inspect an area to ensure it is safe for you to play.) Close to the park, there's also Grand Lake's Winter Carnival every year, featuring snowmobile events, snow sculpture contests, and more.

[DARE TO EXPLORE]

FOSSIL FUN
Visit the most diverse fossil deposits in the world at Florissant Fossil Beds National Monument. Explore 14-foot (4.3-m)-wide petrified redwoods and thousands of detailed insect and plant fossils. About 160 miles (258 km) from the Rockies.
nps.gov/flfo

SWEET RIDE
Head to Ride-a-Kart in nearby Estes Park and have some fun! Challenge your siblings to a go-kart race, hit a homer in the batting cage, and flip out on the bungee trampoline.
rideakart.com

COWBOY SONG
Get a taste for the Old West at a cowboy sing-along! Local musicians perform folk songs around a campfire throughout the summer in downtown Estes Park. Find the dates and times here: cowboybrad.com/shows.html

COOL, DUDE
Hit the Holzwarth Historic Site within the park. Here, you'll find a fully restored dude ranch from the 1920s. Take a tour to see what life was like back then with a guided tour of the property—and a look at the furniture, tools, and other features that welcomed mountain travelers to this spot almost 100 years ago. **(970) 586-1206**

Discover More

4 Handle cool artifacts like animal skins and skulls at the Beaver Meadows Visitor Center (below). While you're there, join a 25-minute ranger talk on the local wildlife and history of the Rockies.

Get in the Saddle

5 Soak in the scenery while riding a horse! Hit the hundreds of miles of horse trails and get the perfect vantage point for wildlife-watching and sightseeing.

MY CHECKLIST
- ✓ Take a drive on Trail Ridge Road.
- ✓ Horseback ride through the park.
- ✓ Check out the sights from the Alpine Visitor Center.
- ✓ Chat with a ranger at Beaver Meadow.
- ✓ Raft down the Colorado River.
- ✓ Snowshoe and sled in the winter.
- ✓ Become a Junior Ranger!

FAST FACT: Rocky Mountain National Park is open 24 hours a day, 365 days a year.

Welcome to Yellowstone National Park!

Arguably the most famous park

in the world, Yellowstone is also the oldest. Established in 1872, Yellowstone falls within three states (Wyoming, Montana, and Idaho) and is bigger than Rhode Island and Delaware combined! Another amazing fact about Yellowstone? There are more geysers and hot springs here than anywhere else on Earth. And it's those gushing geysers combined with the park's vivid views (not to mention wildlife galore!) that make Yellowstone a must-see destination for any fan of the great outdoors.

States: Idaho, Montana, Wyoming
Established: March 1, 1872
Size: 2,221,766 acres (899,118 ha)
Website: nps.gov/yell

DISCOVER YELLOWSTONE

RANGER TIPS

Stay at least 25 yards (22.9 m) away from bison or elk and 100 yards (91.4 m) away from bears and wolves (it's the law). Ask a ranger about geyser schedules so you don't miss an amazing eruption! And make sure to keep your distance from the boiling water of the thermal pools.

TAKE IT EASY

Up for a swim? Head to the swimming hole near Firehole Falls. At a spot where the warm thermal waters mix with the freezing mountain runoff, the temperature is about as perfect as you can get. For a relaxing boat ride, make your way to the Bridge Bay Marina (below), where you can take a boat out to do some sightseeing.

BE EXTREME

Take a soak in the hot spring stream where the Boiling River meets the Gardner River (top left). (Don't worry, the water isn't actually boiling—it's quite comfortable—but make sure to stay in designated soaking spots!)

BEST VIEW

Head out on Canyon Rim Drive to check out great views of the Grand Canyon of Yellowstone and the Yellowstone River's Lower Falls (left). This waterfall is 308 feet (93.9 m) high—that's almost twice the height of Niagara Falls!

ALL ABOUT ANIMALS

Yellowstone is spilling over with wildlife such as elk, wolves (below), moose, bison, bighorn sheep, coyotes, mountain lions, trumpeter swans, grizzly bears, and 280 species of birds. Head to Lamar Valley or Hayden Valley to see some of these animals grazing in the grass. To increase the chance of sighting wildlife, it's best to hit these areas early in the morning or in the evening.

133

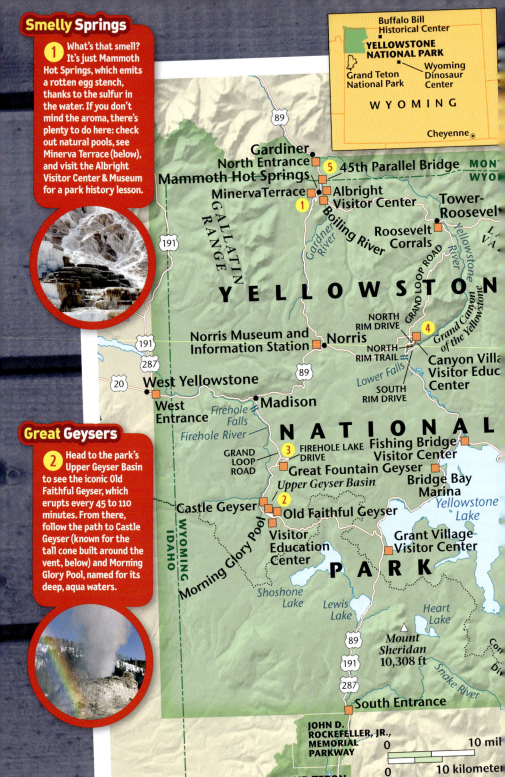

Smelly Springs

1 What's that smell? It's just Mammoth Hot Springs, which emits a rotten egg stench, thanks to the sulfur in the water. If you don't mind the aroma, there's plenty to do here: check out natural pools, see Minerva Terrace (below), and visit the Albright Visitor Center & Museum for a park history lesson.

Great Geysers

2 Head to the park's Upper Geyser Basin to see the iconic Old Faithful Geyser, which erupts every 45 to 110 minutes. From there, follow the path to Castle Geyser (known for the tall cone built around the vent, below) and Morning Glory Pool, named for its deep, aqua waters.

Line It Up

5 Head to the 45th Parallel Bridge, a famed photo-op spot at the border of Montana and Wyoming within the park. Visitors snap shots in front of a sign marking an imaginary line that circles the globe halfway between the Equator and the North Pole (below).

Cool Canyon

4 Yellowstone boasts its own Grand Canyon, a 900-foot (274-m)-deep and half-mile (0.8-m)-wide rocky hole that's definitely a sight to see (below). Head to Canyon Village and the Canyon Rim Trail for an up-close view. While you're here, check out the Canyon Visitor Center for fun exhibits.

Take a Drive

3 Many of Yellowstone's famous sights can be seen from the road. One memorable ride? The Firehole Lake Drive, which offers viewpoints of thermal features like the Great Fountain Geyser, which sometimes shoots steam and water up to 200 feet (61 m) in the air!

[DARE TO EXPLORE]

GRAND ADVENTURE
While you're in Wyoming, you won't want to miss Grand Teton National Park. Go for hikes, hang out at the Kids Ranch, walk around downtown Jackson Hole, and just soak in the sights of the park's magnificent mountain range. **nps.gov/grte**

DINO-MITE
Rated the number one dinosaur museum in the country, Wyoming Dinosaur Center is a must-see for paleontology buffs. See more than 30 mounted skeletons of dinosaurs, check out a dinosaur dig site, and more. About 30 minutes from Yellowstone National Park. **wyodino.org**

ON THE WAGON
Jump into the Wild West with a stagecoach adventure and cookout! Take a ride on a horse-drawn covered wagon, eat some steak prepared by real cowboys, and look for wildlife during a rustic 45-minute ride that leaves from the Roosevelt Corral in Yellowstone. **(866) 439-7375**

HISTORY LESSON
Go back in time at the Buffalo Bill Center of the West. Learn about the American West, Yellowstone natural history, and famous cowboy Buffalo Bill Cody in this museum, located about 100 miles (160.93 km) from Yellowstone. **centerofthewest.org**

MY CHECKLIST
- ✓ Hike around Yellowstone Canyon.
- ✓ Ogle at Old Faithful and other geysers.
- ✓ Snap some pics at the 45th Parallel Bridge.
- ✓ Go swimming near Firehole Falls.
- ✓ Check out exhibits at Yellowstone's museums and visitor centers.
- ✓ Smell the unusual aroma of Mammoth Hot Springs.
- ✓ Keep eyes peeled for animals like bears, elk, and bighorn sheep.

FAST FACT: The Green Dragon Geyser gets its name from the boiling green water it shoots into the sky.

135

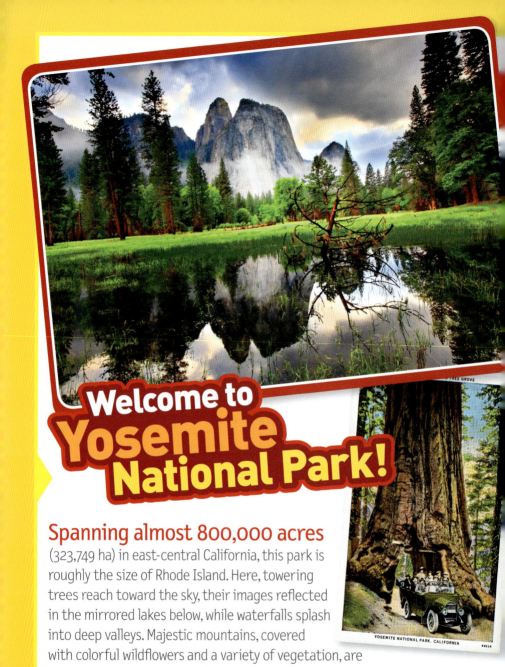

Welcome to Yosemite National Park!

Spanning almost 800,000 acres

(323,749 ha) in east-central California, this park is roughly the size of Rhode Island. Here, towering trees reach toward the sky, their images reflected in the mirrored lakes below, while waterfalls splash into deep valleys. Majestic mountains, covered with colorful wildflowers and a variety of vegetation, are home to an amazing array of wildlife such as the American black bear, spotted owl, mountain lion, and mule deer. Wherever you roam, you'll be blown away by nature's breathtaking beauty. It's no wonder that Yosemite is one of the most popular parks on the planet. From horseback riding to hiking, one thing's for sure: You'll never be bored here!

State: California
Established: October 1, 1890
Size: 761,266 acres (308,074 ha)
Website: nps.gov/yose

DISCOVER YOSEMITE

RANGER TIPS

To beat the crowds, avoid visiting on a holiday weekend, and hit the hiking trails first thing in the morning. Keep your distance from the mule deer, which often come close to humans.

TAKE IT EASY

Take a break from the action by lounging at Sentinel Beach, a wide and sandy picnic area on the Merced River (Cathedral Beach is also a quiet spot). Or hit up the outdoor swimming pool in Curry Village during the summer. If you would rather soak under a waterfall (right), you can do that, too.

BEST VIEWS

Bring your camera to Tunnel View Overlook, said to be the most photographed vista on Earth. Up for a challenge? Take a 3.6-mile (5.8-m) hike to Upper Yosemite Fall and be rewarded with spectacular valley views. Then, at dusk, head to Half Dome (below), where the setting sun casts a gentle glow throughout the eastern end of Yosemite Valley.

BE EXTREME

A magnet for thrill seekers, Yosemite offers one exciting adventure after the next. Within the park you can hang glide off Glacier Point, float down the Merced River in a raft, and rock climb up the famous nose of El Capitan (above). (Note: You need a permit to hang glide.)

ANIMAL SIGHTINGS

A trip to Yosemite just won't be complete without a glimpse of golden-mantled ground squirrels. These chipmunk look-alikes mostly live by the giant sequoia grove. Also watch for Steller's jays (the loudest birds in Yosemite), mule deer, rabbits, coyotes, and maybe even a black bear (pictured here).

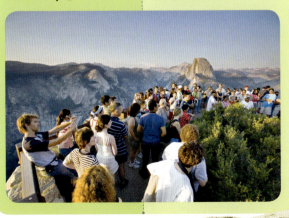

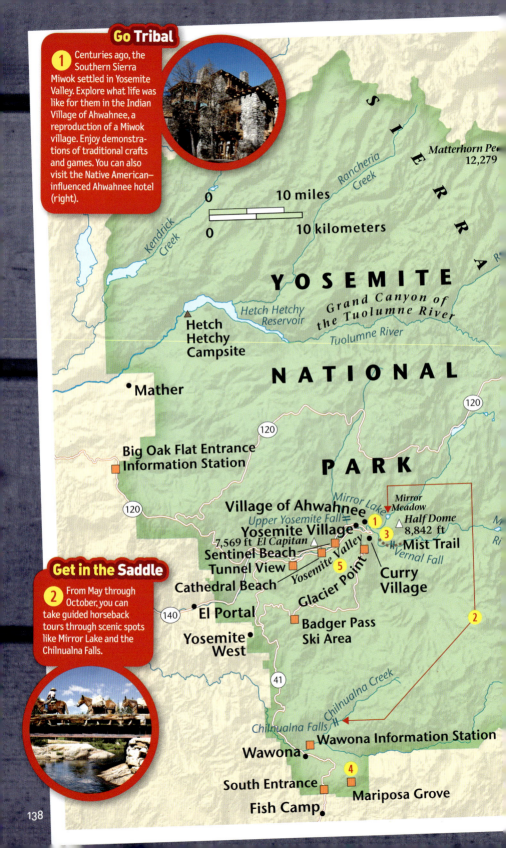

Happy Trails

3 Whether you're up for a tougher trek (like the slippery ascent to the top of Vernal Fall on the Mist Trail) or a simple stroll, some of Yosemite's 800 miles (1,287 km) of marked hiking trails will suit your style.

Ride of a Lifetime

5 Bring your bike (or rent one when you arrive). You can cycle by some of the park's most picturesque spots on the 12 miles (19.3 km) of mostly paved paths circling Yosemite Valley. Hang on to your handlebars!

Tall, Tall Trees

4 Yosemite's famous Mariposa Grove of giant sequoias (left) is home to some of the world's tallest—and oldest—trees. Two must-see trees? The Columbia, which stands taller than the Statue of Liberty, and the Wawona Tunnel Tree.

[DARE TO EXPLORE]

PAN FOR GOLD
Pan for gold in Mariposa, about 30 miles (48.3 km) from Yosemite and you may strike it rich while seeking the shiny stuff in a creek where gold was first found way back in 1848.
goldfeverprospecting.com/gopayo.html

DISCOVER YOUR INNER PHOTOGRAPHER
Learn all about one of America's most well-known photographers at the Ansel Adams Gallery, in the heart of Yosemite Valley. Pick up posters, calendars, and other items featuring Adams's iconic images—plus photography tips from the gallery's staff.
anseladams.com

HIT THE TRACKS
Visit the Yosemite Mountain Sugar Pine Railroad in Fish Camp, near the park's southern entrance. Take a scenic ride through the Sierra Nevada Forest on a historic steam engine, or opt for a quicker trip on the gas-powered Jenny Railcar.
ymsprr.com

GET HANDS-ON
Explore the Children's Museum of the Sierra, located in Oakhurst, about 24 miles (38.6 km) from Yosemite. Visit a kid-size fire station, doctor's office, bank, and pizza restaurant, and other hands-on exhibits.
childrensmuseumofthesierra.com

MY CHECKLIST

- ✓ Check out the rock climbers from El Capitan meadow.
- ✓ Walk to the base of Bridalveil Fall.
- ✓ Meander through Mariposa Grove.
- ✓ Snap some shots from Tunnel View.
- ✓ Gawk at Glacier Point's stunning scenery.
- ✓ Visit the Indian Village of Ahwahnee.
- ✓ Join the Junior Rangers.

FAST FACT: Yosemite's sequoia trees are the largest living things on Earth.

Welcome to Zion National Park!

Zion may not be as famous as some of its national park counterparts, but that doesn't mean it's not as stunning. Within this lesser-explored destination in Utah, you'll find soaring cliffs, rushing waterfalls, deep green natural pools, and red sandstone canyons and rock foundations. Sitting at the junction formed by the Mojave Desert, the Colorado Plateau, and the Great Basin, Zion's unique positioning yields awe-inspiring sights, unique wildlife, and adventures everywhere you go.

State: Utah
Established: November 19, 1919
Size: 146,592 acres (59,324 ha)
Website: nps.gov/zion

DISCOVER ZION

RANGER TIPS

Watch your footing! Zion is filled with steep cliffs and narrow canyons (right), so stay away from the edges. In the summer temperatures can top 105°F (41°C), so be sure to carry plenty of water.

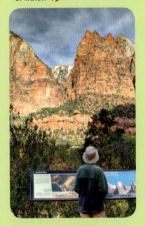

BE EXTREME

Splash and scream down the Virgin River on an inner tube. Part lazy river ride and part water slide, you'll cool off—and get your fill of thrills—by tubing.

BEST VIEW

Hike the one-mile (1.6-km) Canyon Overlook Trail for a magnificent view of lower Zion Canyon (reach the trailhead at the east side of the Zion–Mount Carmel Tunnel). You can also take a drive on the Zion–Mount Carmel Highway and the Zion Canyon Scenic Drive for great views of the park (above left). Note: There is a free shuttle bus from late March to November.

ALL ABOUT ANIMALS

Zion is home to mule deer (below), lizards, ringtails, and rare species like the peregrine falcon, Mexican spotted owl, California condor, desert tortoise, and the endemic Zion snail. Visiting in the late summer or fall? Keep your eyes open for tarantulas, which emerge from their underground homes in search of mates at that time of year.

TAKE IT EASY

Take a break, relax, and eat at the Grotto Picnic Area or under the shade trees near Zion Lodge. For an easy two-mile (3.2-km) stroll head to Riverside Walk, the park's most popular trail. This paved path will lead you past hanging gardens of green maidenhair ferns and golden columbine flowers (below).

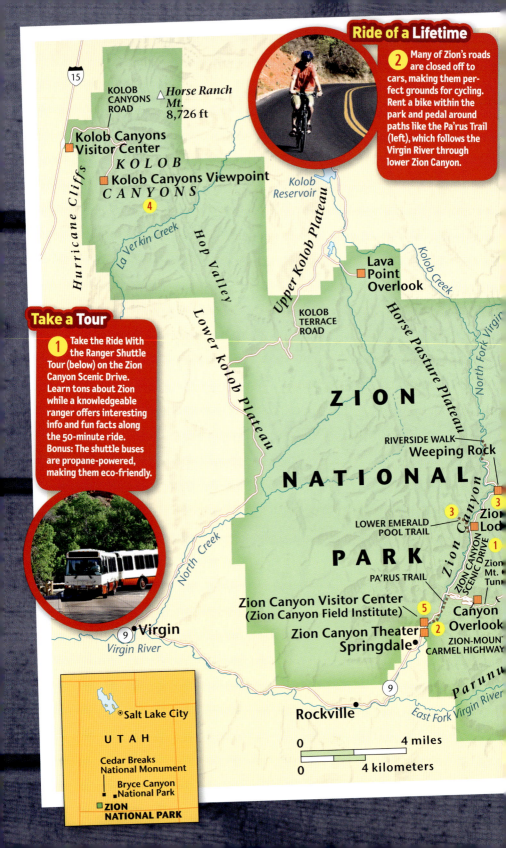

Take a Hike

③ Zion's filled with family-friendly hikes, like the half-mile (0.8-km) round-trip Weeping Rock Trail, where you can actually see water coming out of a rock. The shady and scenic Lower Emerald Pool Trail is another favorite. Up for something a tad tougher? Hit the East Rim, a ten-mile (16.1-km), one-way downhill trail that ends in Zion Canyon.

Get in the Saddle

④ Travel into Kolob Canyon on horseback, just as the pioneers did hundreds of years ago. Take a guided tour and learn from local cowboys, who offer up tales about Zion's sights and wildlife.

Learn More

⑤ Head to the Zion Canyon Field Institute, part of the Zion Natural History Association, where you can join an outdoor workshop on topics like photography and geology or link up with guided tours.

[DARE TO EXPLORE]

HIT THE BREAKS
Travel to Cedar Breaks National Monument, about 75 miles (121 km) north of Zion National Park, to see sculpted hoodoos, spires, and colorful wildflowers in the spring. **nps.gov/cebr**

PARK HOP
Double your park fun by hitting Bryce Canyon National Park, about 50 miles (80.5 km) away from Zion. Once you get there, take the Bryce Canyon shuttle around the park.
nps.gov/brca

RAINY DAY?
Or maybe you just need to rest your legs after all of that hiking. In either case, stop at the Zion Canyon Giant Screen Theater for a few hours of fun. See a 3-D movie on the six-story-high, 82-foot (25-m)-wide screen.
zioncanyontheatre.com

PIT STOP
Learn even more about the park at the Zion Canyon Visitor Center. It features a huge bookstore and cool exhibits; you can also shop for souvenirs, pick up park maps, and chat with rangers to better plan your time in Zion.
nps.gov/zion/naturescience/zion-canyon-visitor-center.htm

EAST RIM TRAIL

 East Entrance

MY CHECKLIST
✓ Take a bike ride through the park.
✓ Cruise along the sites on the park shuttle.
✓ Ride down a canyon on horseback.
✓ Tube down the Virgin River.
✓ View the algae-green Emerald Pools.
✓ Check out the Weeping Rock.
✓ Head to the Zion Canyon Visitor Center for exhibits and info.

FAST FACT: The park's 287-foot (87.5-m)-long Kolob Arch is one of the world's largest freestanding natural arches.

143

CENTENNIAL EDITION

BY THE NUMBERS!
RECORD SETTERS IN THE NATIONAL PARKS

Biggest, tallest, hottest, lowest: Our national parks are not only natural wonders—they're record setters! Check out the titles that these parks hold.

20,320 FEET (6,194 M)
THE FEAT: Highest Point in North America
THE PLACE: Mount McKinley, Denali National Park & Preserve

Rising from the Alaska Range, Mount McKinley is a block of granite that is half covered in permanent snowfields. It was given its name by a prospector in honor of U.S. President William McKinley, but it is also known by its Athabaskan Indian name: Denali, which means "Great One."

400 MILES (644 KM)
THE FEAT: Longest Known Cave System in the World
THE PLACE: Mammoth Cave system, Mammoth Cave National Park

Some 400 miles (644 km) of Kentucky's Mammoth Cave system have been explored, but no one really knows how far it extends, as new caverns continue to be discovered. Over 4,000 years ago, the first humans entered the cave, which contains more than 1,000 stalactite formations.

134°F (57°C)
THE FEAT: Hottest Place on Earth
THE PLACE: Death Valley National Park

Death Valley holds the record for world's highest air temperature—recorded at Furnace Creek in 1913. It's also the lowest place in North America—the park's Badwater Basin is 282 feet (86 m) below sea level. The average annual rainfall in Death Valley, which is located in California and Nevada, is less than two inches (5 cm), making it the driest place in North America.

144

379 FEET (116 M)

THE FEAT: World's Tallest Trees

THE PLACE: Redwood National Park

Coast redwoods—the world's tallest trees—grow on the Northern California coast and the southernmost coast of Oregon. They are the stars of Redwood National Park. The towering trees can live to be 2,000 years old.

OVER 290 FEET (88 M) TALL AND 275 FEET (84 M) LONG

THE FEAT: World's Largest Natural Bridge

THE PLACE: Rainbow Bridge National Monument

You have to crane your neck to see over this rainbow. The pink sandstone Rainbow Bridge, located in Utah, spans across a canyon above a creek that makes its way to Lake Powell.

4 MILLION POUNDS (1.8 MILLION KG)

THE FEAT: Largest Living Tree

THE PLACE: Sequoia National Park

With a name like General Sherman, it's easy to take this enormous tree seriously. Standing 271 feet (82.6 m) tall in California's Sequoia National Park, it is the largest tree on Earth by volume. Believed to be 2,200 years old, the weight of the giant sequoia, including the roots, is the same as four Boeing 747 jets.

10,099,276 people

THE FEAT: Most Visited National Park

THE PLACE: Great Smoky Mountains National Park

Attracting more than 10 million visitors per year, Great Smoky Mountains is the nation's busiest national park! Its central location in North Carolina and Tennessee is within a day or two's drive for two-thirds of the U.S. population. Famous for its diversity of plant and animal life, the park is home to some 65 species of mammals, more than 200 varieties of birds, 67 native fish species, and more than 80 types of reptiles and amphibians!

On top of that, Great Smoky Mountains is known as the "Salamander Capital of the World" because the world's most diverse population of salamanders—at least 30 different species—lives there!

▸ Other Must-see Park Properties in the West

ALA KAHAKAI NATIONAL HISTORIC TRAIL (HI)

nps.gov/alka

WHY IT'S COOL: It's a 175-mile (282-km) trail through hundreds of ancient Hawaiian settlement sites.

WHAT TO DO: Hiking and exploring the temples, house site foundations, fishponds, fishing shrines, petroglyphs, sacred places, ponds, and reefs.

TRY THIS: Look for sea turtles along the shores of Anaehoomalu and Makaiwa Bays.

BIGHORN CANYON NATIONAL RECREATION AREA (MT, WY)

nps.gov/bica

WHY IT'S COOL: It has steep canyon walls and is home to a diversity of wildlife, including wild horses, black bears, bighorn rams, and mule deer.

WHAT TO DO: Visit historic ranches; boating, hiking, and wildlife-watching.

TRY THIS: Take your bike along South District park road, paralleling the ancient Bad Pass Trail.

CABRILLO NATIONAL MONUMENT (CA)

nps.gov/cabr

WHY IT'S COOL: It's the site where the first Europeans set foot on what is now the West Coast of the United States.

WHAT TO DO: Visit Old Point Loma Lighthouse; hiking, bird-watching, tide-pooling, and biking.

TRY THIS: Take a walk to the Whale Overlook to see views of the Pacific and, in winter, whales.

CEDAR BREAKS NATIONAL MONUMENT (UT)

nps.gov/cebr

WHY IT'S COOL: It features multicolored rock formations—some 60 million years old.

WHAT TO DO: Hiking, camping, and scenic drives.

TRY THIS: Learn about the monument's amazing geology through ranger programs.

COLORADO NATIONAL MONUMENT (CO)

nps.gov/colm

WHY IT'S COOL: Its grand panorama of plateau and canyon offers one of the most beautiful landscapes in the West.

WHAT TO DO: Hiking, camping, bicycling, rock climbing, and wildlife-watching.

TRY THIS: Take in the scenery and red-rock canyons along the 23-mile (37-km) Rim Rock Drive.

CRATERS OF THE MOON NATIONAL MONUMENT AND PRESERVE (ID)

nps.gov/crmo

WHY IT'S COOL: Rugged lava flows that resemble the surface of the moon.

WHAT TO DO: Climb a volcano; take a ranger-led tour; camping, hiking, backpacking, skiing, and snowshoeing.

TRY THIS: Take in exceptional views from your car by driving the seven-mile (11.3-km) loop.

DEVILS TOWER NATIONAL MONUMENT (WY)

nps.gov/deto

WHY IT'S COOL: It's home to Devils Tower, an amazing geologic formation created by the intrusion of igneous material.

WHAT TO DO: Hiking trails, rock climbing, and cross-country skiing.

TRY THIS: Take the Tower Walk, which explores Devils Tower with a ranger.

DINOSAUR NATIONAL MONUMENT (CO, UT)

nps.gov/dino

WHY IT'S COOL: Tons of skeletons and skulls and other specimens of Jurassic-period dinosaurs have been found here.

WHAT TO DO: View rock art left by the people of the Fremont culture; hiking, camping, stargazing, and boating.

TRY THIS: Discover the park's river canyons by taking a raft trip down the Green and Yampa Rivers.

FORT VANCOUVER NATIONAL HISTORIC SITE (OR, WA)

nps.gov/fova

WHY IT'S COOL: This site preserves and re-creates a story of the 19th-century fur trading network.

WHAT TO DO: Tour the reconstructed trading post and attend park ranger weapons demonstrations and living history programs.

TRY THIS: Watch a cultural demonstration to learn about people, events, and practices of the past.

FOSSIL BUTTE NATIONAL MONUMENT (WY)

nps.gov/fobu

WHY IT'S COOL: One of the world's most abundant, detailed, and best preserved deposits of Eocene-epoch fossils.

WHAT TO DO: View fossil exhibits, take a scenic drive, join a ranger program, and assist on fossil collections.

TRY THIS: Have a picnic under the shade of aspen trees at the Chicken Creek Picnic Area.

GOLDEN GATE NATIONAL RECREATION AREA (CA)

nps.gov/goga

WHY IT'S COOL: Endless sights to see and things to do, like the Muir Woods National Monument, Fort Point National Historic Site, the Presidio, Nike Missile Site, and Ocean Beach.

WHAT TO DO: Visit the sights and tour historic areas and structures; hiking, swimming, camping, picnicking, and wildlife-watching.

TRY THIS: Take a boat ride to Alcatraz Island and see what life was like for prisoners who lived on "the Rock" from 1934 to 1963.

HOVENWEEP NATIONAL MONUMENT (CO, UT)

nps.gov/hove

WHY IT'S COOL: It protects the remains of six prehistoric Puebloan-era villages along the Utah–Colorado border.

WHAT TO DO: Tour the ancient Pueblo ruins; join a ranger-led program; hiking and camping.

TRY THIS: Stay past dark and check out the stars above Hovenweep, which still twinkle as bright today as they did 700 years ago!

KLONDIKE GOLD RUSH NATIONAL HISTORICAL PARK (AK)

nps.gov/klgo

WHY IT'S COOL: It tells the story of the great Yukon gold rush of 1897.

WHAT TO DO: Tour historic buildings and boom-towns; hiking and camping.

TRY THIS: Ride the historic White Pass & Yukon Railroad for stunning views of the Coast Mountains.

LAKE MEAD NATIONAL RECREATION AREA (AZ, NV)

nps.gov/lake

WHY IT'S COOL: It's home to Lake Mead and Lake Mohave, plus acres of desert and wilderness.

WHAT TO DO: Boating, kayaking, canoeing, waterskiing, hiking, fishing, picnicking, plus exploring mountains, desert basins, and canyons.

TRY THIS: Hot day? Take a dip in the sparkling clean waters of Lake Mead and Lake Mohave.

LAKE ROOSEVELT NATIONAL RECREATION AREA (WA)

nps.gov/laro

WHY IT'S COOL: It provides visitors with tons of recreational opportunities along and on the beautiful river.

WHAT TO DO: Camping, boating, fishing, swimming, picnicking, and hiking.

TRY THIS: Tour the grounds of historic Fort Spokane, a U.S. military post and an Indian boarding school.

LITTLE BIGHORN BATTLEFIELD NATIONAL MONUMENT (MT)

nps.gov/libi

WHY IT'S COOL: It's the site of Lt. Col. George A. Custer's "last stand" and a monument to the Sioux and Cheyenne Indians who battled there.

WHAT TO DO: Tour the battlefield and the Custer National Cemetery.

TRY THIS: Head to the visitor center and stick around for ranger-led talks on the battlefields and history.

MUIR WOODS NATIONAL MONUMENT (CA)

nps.gov/muwo

WHY IT'S COOL: You'll see redwood trees up to 260 feet (79.2 m) tall, averaging 600 to 800 years of age.

WHAT TO DO: Gaze up at the giant redwoods, hike some of the park's miles of trails, learn about its diverse flora and fauna, and go on ranger-led tours.

TRY THIS: Hike the Marin Headlands, where you'll find Fort Cronkhite, a former World War II military post at the edge of the Pacific Ocean.

OREGON CAVES NATIONAL MONUMENT AND PRESERVE (OR)

nps.gov/orca

WHY IT'S COOL: It's home to one of the few marble caves in the world!

WHAT TO DO: Cave tours, hiking, and ranger-led programs.

TRY THIS: Hit one of the park's four hiking trails to check out views of the surrounding Siskiyou Mountains.

PUʻUHONUA O HŌNAUNAU NATIONAL HISTORICAL PARK (HI)

nps.gov/puho

WHY IT'S COOL: It provides a window into Hawaii's past, where the traditional life of Hawaiians is preserved and shared.

WHAT TO DO: Touring historic structures; fishing, hiking, snorkeling, wildlife-watching, and picnicking.

TRY THIS: Take a self-guided walking tour of the Royal Grounds and Puʻuhonua, offering a glimpse of how ancient Hawaiians lived.

SAN JUAN ISLAND NATIONAL HISTORICAL PARK (WA)

nps.gov/sajh

WHY IT'S COOL: In 1859, the United States and Great Britain almost went to war when an American farmer shot a pig here, also home to more than six miles (9.6 km) of shoreline.

WHAT TO DO: Hike the trails at English and American camps; study artifacts in the American Camp visitor center; kayaking, bird-watching, whale-watching, stargazing, and picking blackberries.

TRY THIS: Go tide-pooling! American Camp along the Strait of Juan de Fuca has plenty of pocket coves full of mollusks, crabs, shrimp, and more.

SANTA MONICA MOUNTAINS NATIONAL RECREATION AREA (CA)

nps.gov/samo

WHY IT'S COOL: Amazing mountain peaks, sandy beaches, rugged coastline, and plenty of trails, too.

WHAT TO DO: Visit historic sites; hiking, camping, and mountain biking.

TRY THIS: Check out the park on horseback by hitting some of the more than 500 miles (805 km) of horse trails.

WAR IN THE PACIFIC NATIONAL HISTORICAL PARK (GU)

nps.gov/wapa

WHY IT'S COOL: It's a memorial to the bravery and sacrifice of the soldiers and civilians who participated in World War II's Pacific Theater.

WHAT TO DO: Visit battlefield and other historical sites; diving and snorkeling.

TRY THIS: Head up to Asan Bay Overlook for a panoramic view and its Memorial Wall, which contains 17,771 names of soldiers who suffered or died during the war on Guam.

WORLD WAR II VALOR IN THE PACIFIC NATIONAL MONUMENT (AK, CA, HI)

nps.gov/valr

WHY IT'S COOL: It honors those who died in the December 7, 1941, attack on the U.S. Navy base at Pearl Harbor.

WHAT TO DO: Visit the battleship memorial and battle sites, tour the museum galleries, and explore exhibits.

TRY THIS: Hop on a bike and follow the nearby Pearl Harbor bike path, which crosses through Aiea Bay park.

National Park of American Samoa

A diver swims among beautiful corals in the crystal blue water off the coast of Ofu Island in the National Park of American Samoa.

more National Parks
& Park Properties

◆◆ More National Parks and Park Properties

AMERICAN SAMOA, NATIONAL PARK OF

American Samoa
Established October 31, 1988
10,520 acres (4,257 ha)
nps.gov/npsa

RANGER TIPS
- Want to snorkel? Bring your own equipment since beaches are remote.
- Watch for falling coconuts!
- Avoid stepping on or touching coral.

TAKE IT EASY: Spend a day relaxing at the secluded Ofu Beach.

BEST VIEW: Climb to the top of Mount Alava to get a great glimpse of the harbor and town of Pago Pago.

BE EXTREME: Explore coral reefs by snorkeling in the waters off the Ofu and Olosega beaches.

ANIMAL SIGHTINGS: Samoan flying foxes, fruit doves, and tropical fish

ARCHES NATIONAL PARK

Utah
Established November 12, 1971
76,359 acres (30,901 ha)
nps.gov/arch

RANGER TIPS
- Stay on trails to protect fragile desert soils and plants.
- Wear supportive shoes and watch your footing; sandstone slickrock crumbles easily.
- Don't forget your water! You'll want to drink at least a gallon (4 L) a day while hiking.

TAKE IT EASY: Head to the Windows area for a series of short, easy hikes.

BEST VIEW: Stop at the Park Avenue Viewpoint for a view down an open canyon and sandstone skyscrapers.

BE EXTREME: Join the naturalist-led three-hour hike through Fiery Furnace, a dense array of rock formations that glow red as the sun sets.

ANIMAL SIGHTINGS: Mule deer, black-tailed jackrabbits, coyotes, and lizards

BISCAYNE NATIONAL PARK

Florida
Established June 28, 1980
172,924 acres (69,980 ha)
nps.gov/bisc

RANGER TIPS
- Don't touch coral or anything else living on the reef.
- Bring your bug spray! Mosquitoes are plentiful from April to December.
- Access to anything beyond the mainland shoreline of Biscayne requires a boat ride.

TAKE IT EASY: Enjoy a picnic along the Mangrove Shore at Convoy Point.

BEST VIEW: Check out life underneath Biscayne Bay on a reef cruise via glass-bottom boat.

BE EXTREME: Snorkel in the shallow waters and check out life on a coral reef.

ANIMAL SIGHTINGS: Shrimp, spiny lobsters, sponges, crabs, Florida manatees, and more than 325 types of fish

BLACK CANYON OF THE GUNNISON NATIONAL PARK

Colorado
Established October 21, 1999
30,385 acres (12,296 ha)
nps.gov/blca

RANGER TIPS
- Bring lots of water; the park's exposed trails heat up in the sun during the summer.
- If you plan to hike the inner canyon routes, you must get a permit from the visitor center first.
- Never throw anything into the canyon.

TAKE IT EASY: Follow the Rim Rock Nature Trail, a one-mile (1.6-km) round-trip trek offering views of the river and canyon below.

BEST VIEW: Hit High Point on the South Rim and stand 2,689 feet (820 m) above the Gunnison River.

BE EXTREME: Rock climb some of the park's cliffs and canyons.

ANIMAL SIGHTINGS: Ravens, falcons, peregrine falcons, mule deer, elk, bobcats, mountain lions, and black bears

CANYONLANDS NATIONAL PARK

Utah
Established September 12, 1964
337,598 acres (136,621 ha)
nps.gov/cany

RANGER TIPS
- The spring and fall are ideal seasons for exploring by foot or car.
- Be extra careful around cliff edges and on slippery surfaces.
- Don't walk on the crunchy black soil seen in the park; it's composed of living plants.

TAKE IT EASY: The road to Upheaval Dome ends at a perfect picnic spot in the shade of junipers and pinyon trees.

BEST VIEW: At 6,080 feet (1,853 m), Grand View Point Overlook offers sweeping views of the canyons.

BE EXTREME: Bike through the park's backcountry, which is closed to cars. Check out The Needles, a collection of weathered sandstone spires.

ANIMAL SIGHTINGS: Mule deer, coyotes, porcupines, and lizards

CAPITOL REEF NATIONAL PARK

Utah
Established December 18, 1971
241,904 acres (97,895 ha)
nps.gov/care

RANGER TIPS
- Always check road, trail, and weather conditions before you head out on foot or by car.
- Carry in your own water, which is scarce once you enter the park.
- Pack a picnic! There's no place to buy food in the park.

TAKE IT EASY: Stop at the visitor center on the edge of Fruita to see remnants of a 120-year-old frontier community.

BEST VIEW: A 2.5-mile (4-km) hike to Strike Valley Overlook in the upper Muley Twist Canyon will lead you to a vista of a canyon, double arches, and a large rock window.

BE EXTREME: Hit the Cohab Canyon Trail. This almost 2-mile (3.2-km) hike is considered strenuous, but you'll get to climb to a hidden canyon that overlooks Fruita.

ANIMAL SIGHTINGS: Mule deer, bighorn sheep, and soaring golden eagles

CHANNEL ISLANDS NATIONAL PARK

California
Established March 5, 1980
249,354 acres (100,910 ha)
nps.gov/chis

RANGER TIPS
- Want to whale-watch? Hit the park from late December through March.
- Do not take anything from the boat but photos.
- Dress in layers for all types of weather.

TAKE IT EASY: Hit the beach of San Miguel, home to five seal species.

BEST VIEW: Climb the staircase to the top of the cliff on Anacapa Island and peer 150 feet (45.7 m) below to the sea.

BE EXTREME: Take a bumpy boat ride on the Santa Barbara Channel out to Anacapa Island.

ANIMAL SIGHTINGS: Seabirds, seals, sea lions, rabbits, and lizards

CONGAREE NATIONAL PARK

South Carolina
Established 2003
26,546 acres (10,743 ha)
nps.gov/cong

RANGER TIPS
- Bring bug spray to ward off mosquitoes.
- Avoid all snakes—there are poisonous species in the park.
- Bring an extra set of clothes to change into after your visit—you'll probably get muddy!

TAKE IT EASY: Hit the park at night for the ranger-led "owl prowl" to hear the eerie *hoo-hoos* of owls and see the glowing fungi that grows on cypress trees.

BEST VIEW: Take the 2.4-mile (3.9-km) Boardwalk Trail to see some of the country's tallest trees, like giant loblolly pines and old bald cypresses.

BE EXTREME: Paddle the Cedar Creek Canoe Trail and look for wildlife in the water.

ANIMAL SIGHTINGS: Bobcats, deer, river otters, woodpeckers, owls, turtles, and wild pigs

DRY TORTUGAS NATIONAL PARK

Florida
Established October 26, 1992
64,657 acres (26,166 ha)
nps.gov/drto

RANGER TIPS
- Avoid travel to the park during hurricane season (June through November).
- Want to snorkel? The visitor center has goggles, snorkels, and flippers available for loan.
- Bring your own water and food—there is nothing available within the park.

TAKE IT EASY: Stroll the grassy parapet at the Garden Key harbor light, where you can check out huge coastal guns.

BEST VIEW: Climb the spiral staircase to the top of Fort Jefferson for 360-degree views—and awesome bird-watching.

BE EXTREME: Snorkel along the 0.6-mile (1-km) seawall and moat, or swim from the beach to isolated Bush Key (check with the visitor center first to make sure the key is open).

ANIMAL SIGHTINGS: Queen conch, yellow stingrays, gray snappers, sea stars, and 442 species of fish

GATES OF THE ARCTIC NATIONAL PARK AND PRESERVE

Alaska
Established December 2, 1980
8,472,506 acres (3,428,707 ha)
nps.gov/gaar

RANGER TIPS
- Layer up! The weather is unpredictable and you can expect snow or rain at any time.
- There are no visitor centers here, so bring everything you may need with you.
- Stick to the trails and avoid stepping on the fragile lichen, which takes 150 years to grow.

TAKE IT EASY: Because it's so rugged, Gates of the Arctic is recommended for highly skilled hikers only.

BEST VIEW: Climb practically any ridge of the park to see spectacular scenes of glaciers, mountains, alpine valleys, and forested lowlands.

BE EXTREME: Float down the Alatna River on a four-to-seven-day wilderness trip.

ANIMAL SIGHTINGS: Caribou, grizzly bears, wolves, wolverines, foxes, and gyrfalcons

GLACIER BAY NATIONAL PARK AND PRESERVE

Alaska
Established December 2, 1980
3,280,198 acres (1,327,451 ha)
nps.gov/glba

RANGER TIPS
- Be careful—brown bears are common, especially on Blue Mouse Cove.
- Do not get close to icebergs when boating.
- Never climb on a glacier without a guide.

TAKE IT EASY: Follow the Bartlett River Trail through a rain forest to a quiet meadow.

BEST VIEW: Go to the bay's west arm to see stunning views of the 15,300-foot (4,663-m) Mount Fairweather.

BE EXTREME: Paddle around the bay's Muir and Adams Inlets, favorite spots of kayakers.

ANIMAL SIGHTINGS: Wolves, moose, mountain goats, bears, bald eagles, harbor seals, humpback whales, killer whales, and birds

GREAT BASIN NATIONAL PARK

Nevada
Established October 27, 1986
77,180 acres (31,234 ha)
nps.gov/grba

RANGER TIPS
- Beware of sudden thunderstorms that pop up any time of the year.
- Early in the morning is the best time to view Wheeler Peak.
- Stay on marked roads and trails to avoid damaging fragile alpine plants.

155

TAKE IT EASY: Follow a short trail to the historical Osceola Ditch, built in the late 1880s to carry water for gold mining.

BEST VIEW: Pull off at the Peak Overlook for awesome views of Wheeler Peak, dropping 1,800 feet (549 m) to a glacier below.

BE EXTREME: Explore the intricate underground passages at Lehman Caves.

ANIMAL SIGHTINGS: Pack rats, cave crickets, snakes, and the rare pseudoscorpion—a spider with scorpion-like pinchers.

GUADALUPE MOUNTAINS NATIONAL PARK

Texas
Established September 30, 1972
86,416 acres (34,971 ha)
nps.gov/gumo

RANGER TIPS
- Pick up maps and trail information at the Headquarters Visitor Center.
- Canyon plants are fragile; be sure to stay on the trails.
- Keep your eye open for harmful desert animals like rattlesnakes.

TAKE IT EASY: Walk the easy 2.3-mile (3.7-km) loop trail to Smith and Manzanita Springs to familiarize yourself with the plants of the Chihuahuan Desert.

BEST VIEWS: Take the Bush Mountain Trail, leading to spectacular views of the Guadalupes and the Cornudas Mountains.

BE EXTREME: Hike Devil's Hall, a 4.3-mile (6.9-km) round-trip trek down a steep, narrow canyon.

ANIMAL SIGHTINGS: Snakes, golden eagles, tarantulas (in the fall), and hummingbirds

ISLE ROYALE NATIONAL PARK

Michigan
Established April 3, 1940
571,790 acres (231,396 ha)
nps.gov/isro

RANGER TIPS
- Pack in what you need and carry out your waste and trash.
- Any water collected in the park must be boiled or filtered before you drink it.
- The best way to see the park is by backpacking to campsites; noncampers can explore on tour boats or on foot.

TAKE IT EASY: Visiting in July or August? Pick blueberries and thimbleberries in the park's lush green meadows.

BEST VIEWS: Climb to Scoville Point to view some of the rocky islets that form the beautiful Isle Royale archipelago.

BE EXTREME: Take a three-to-five-day backpacking trip into the backcountry to see exclusive sights of the park.

ANIMAL SIGHTINGS: Wolves, moose, and foxes

KATMAI NATIONAL PARK AND PRESERVE

Alaska
Established December 2, 1980
4,725,188 acres (1,912,219 ha)
nps.gov/katm

RANGER TIPS
- Stick to the bear-viewing platforms—never go near a bear.
- Be extra careful when crossing glacial streams.
- Always kayak with a guide.

TAKE IT EASY: Take the bus or van tour to the Valley of Ten Thousand Smokes to see stunning scenery.

BEST VIEW: Watch bears feeding on jumping fish from the platform at Brooks Falls.

BE EXTREME: Kayak or canoe in the Bay of Islands in the North Arm of Naknek Lake.

ANIMAL SIGHTINGS: Alaskan brown bears, gray wolves, moose, caribou, porcupines, beavers, sea lions, sea otters, and hair seals. You may also spot beluga, killer, and gray whales along the coast.

KENAI FJORDS NATIONAL PARK

Alaska
Established December 2, 1980
607,000 acres (245,645 ha)
nps.gov/kefj

RANGER TIPS
- Kenai's icefields are very cold year-round. Dress appropriately.
- Respect the glaciers by keeping your distance. Remember, they're moving bodies of ice and parts may break off.
- Beware of brown bears and moose.

TAKE IT EASY: Take a boat tour down Resurrection Bay and look for sea lions as you pass the Chiswell Islands.

BEST VIEW: Follow the Main Trail from the Seward Information Center for glacier and icefield views.

BE EXTREME: Kayak the Granite Passage, an exciting entrance into Harris Bay.

ANIMAL SIGHTINGS: Harbor seals, sea lions, sea otters, moose, black bears, mountain goats, wolverines, lynx, bald eagles, puffins, peregrine falcons, and about 20 species of seabirds

KINGS CANYON NATIONAL PARK

California
Established March 4, 1940
461,901 acres (186,925 ha)
nps.gov/seki

RANGER TIPS
- Watch your footing around rivers and streams. The rocks can be very slippery.
- Look out for falling pinecones!
- You may gather a few pinecones or rocks from the Sequoia National Forest area only. Taking items from Kings Canyon is not allowed.

TAKE IT EASY: Walk or bike to Cedar Grove Village, a beautiful hidden valley.

BEST VIEW: Drive up to Panoramic Point to see stretches of the Sierra Nevada and the Great Western Divide.

BE EXTREME: Explore the marble Crystal Cave via a twisting, one-hour underground tour.

ANIMAL SIGHTINGS: Marmots, pikas, gray foxes, bobcats, striped and spotted skunks, black bears, birds, snakes, and lizards

KOBUK VALLEY NATIONAL PARK

Alaska
Established December 2, 1980
1,750,000 acres (708,201 ha)
nps.gov/kova

RANGER TIPS
- Bring everything you need with you—there are no facilities.

- Take a guide along unless you are very experienced in the wilderness.
- Respect the activities of the Inuit people, who own much of the land along the river.

TAKE IT EASY: Take an easy canoe ride down the wide and gentle Kobuk River.

BEST VIEW: Climb to the top of the Great Kobuk Sand Dunes for a look at the amazing landscape.

BE EXTREME: Take a river-hiking trip.

ANIMAL SIGHTINGS: Brown bears, black bears, wolves, coyotes, and foxes

LAKE CLARK NATIONAL PARK AND PRESERVE

Alaska
Established December 2, 1980
4,030,006 acres (1,630,888 ha)
nps.gov/lacl

RANGER TIPS
- Hit Lake Clark in the summer to see its beautiful (and famous) wildflowers.
- Plan ahead—you can only reach this park by boat or air taxi.
- Experienced hikers only: You have to have good wilderness skills to hike, camp, or fish here.

TAKE IT EASY: Lake Clark fishing is top-notch. Cast your line into the lakes or river and relax while waiting for fish (like trout and five kinds of salmon) to bite.

BEST VIEW: Climb the 2.5-mile (4-km) Tanalian Falls Trail through a forest, past bogs, and up a river to see these stunning falls.

BE EXTREME: Take a two-day rafting trip down the wild and scenic Tanalian or Tazimina Rivers.

ANIMAL SIGHTINGS: Moose, arctic ground squirrels, caribou, coyotes, wolves, lynx, river otters, wolverines, and 215 species of birds. Look for sea lions, beluga whales, harbor seals, and porpoises in the nearby bays.

LASSEN VOLCANIC NATIONAL PARK

California
Established August 9, 1916
106,448 acres (43,078 ha)
nps.gov/lavo

RANGER TIPS
- View the volcanoes in the summer and fall.
- Carry water, wear a hat, and take a jacket.
- Before you set out on a hike, take some time to acclimate to the park's high elevations.

TAKE IT EASY: Visit the Loomis Museum at Manzanita Lake to learn more about the area.

BEST VIEW: Drive the park's main road for up-close looks at the park's volcanic features.

BE EXTREME: Hike the Lassen Peak Trail, a tough five-mile (8-km) round-trip climb that brings you to 8,463 feet (2,580 km) at the summit of the active volcano.

ANIMAL SIGHTINGS: Ground squirrels, tortoiseshell butterflies, frogs, newts, and 195 species of birds

MAMMOTH CAVE NATIONAL PARK

Kentucky
Established July 1, 1941
52,830 acres (21,380 ha)
nps.gov/maca

RANGER TIPS
- Wear shoes with nonskid soles and long pants while exploring the cave.
- Temperatures in the cave are cool, so bring an extra layer of clothing.
- Cave tours are tough. Make sure you're up to the task before starting your journey.

TAKE IT EASY: Stop for lunch at the Snowball Room in the Cleveland Avenue section, featuring snowball-like formations on the roof.

BEST VIEW: Stare into the 105-foot (32-m)-deep Bottomless Pit.

BE EXTREME: Sign up for the Wild Cave Tour, a five-mile (8-km), six-hour, belly-crawling journey into the cave.

ANIMAL SIGHTINGS: Deer, bobcats, foxes, muskrats, flying squirrels, raccoons, skunks, mink, lizards, turtles, snakes, salamanders, toads, frogs, lizards, and many birds

MESA VERDE NATIONAL PARK

Colorado
Established June 29, 1906
52,074 acres (21,074 ha)
nps.gov/meve

RANGER TIPS

- Bring binoculars! They'll come in handy when you want to peer across the canyons.
- Visiting the cliff dwellings? Wear sturdy shoes and be prepared for some tough climbs.
- Never get too close to the edge of cliff trails and canyon rims.

TAKE IT EASY: Visit the Chapin Mesa Museum for guides to the major sites and exhibits about the Mesa Verde people.

BEST VIEW: Drive to Sun Point Overlook to see a bunch of cliff dwellings, like Cliff Palace, Sunset House, and Mummy House.

BE EXTREME: Scale a 32-foot (9.8-m) ladder to reach Balcony House, a 40-room dwelling that requires a crawl through a tunnel to exit.

ANIMAL SIGHTINGS: Coyotes, gray foxes, mountain lions, black bears, elk, marmots, porcupines, jackrabbits, and owls

NORTH CASCADES NATIONAL PARK

Washington
Established October 2, 1968
684,000 acres (276,805 ha)
nps.gov/noca

RANGER TIPS

- Summer gives you the best access to the park and its activities.
- Bring binoculars to spot climbers and mountain goats on the granite faces of the Cascade peaks.
- Boat tours require a reservation; make yours at least a month in advance.

TAKE IT EASY: Take City Light's 2.5-hour boat tour of Diablo Lake.

BEST VIEW: Stop at the Washington Pass Overlook for an amazing view of Cascade peaks, including the 7,740-foot (2,359-m) Early Winter Spires.

BE EXTREME: Take the rugged and steep Horseshoe Basin Trail, a 3.9-mile (6.3-km) trek passing more than 15 waterfalls as glaciers and mountains loom in the background.

ANIMAL SIGHTINGS: Columbia black-tailed deer, Douglas squirrels, pikas, mountain goats, reptiles, amphibians, and bald eagles

SAGUARO NATIONAL PARK

Arizona
Established October 14, 1994
91,445 acres (37,007 ha)
nps.gov/sagu

RANGER TIPS
- Always stay on the trails.
- If out at night, carry a flashlight to avoid encounters with unsuspecting wildlife.
- Pack plenty of water and snacks for hikes.

TAKE IT EASY: Grab lunch and check out centuries-old petroglyphs etched in the rocks in the Signal Hill Picnic Area.

BEST VIEWS: Head to the top of Valley View Overlook Trail to get a great view of the cactus-covered land below.

BE EXTREME: Hop on a mountain bike and pedal your way down Cactus Forest Trail, a 2.5-mile (4-km) dirt trail rolling by desert scrub and sagebrush.

ANIMAL SIGHTINGS: Desert tortoises, desert iguanas, horned lizards, Gila monsters, six species of rattlesnakes, and black bears

SEQUOIA NATIONAL PARK

California
Established September 25, 1890
404,063 acres (163,519 ha)
nps.gov/seki

RANGER TIPS
- Hit the trails and take a hike for the park's best vantage points.
- Pack a magnifying glass in your backpack so you can see some of the smaller things living in Sequoia.
- Wear layers and bring a jacket with you—the weather and temperatures can vary throughout the park.
- Avoid run-ins with wildlife by keeping your food properly stored and picking up all of your trash.

TAKE IT EASY: Stroll the Congress Trail, which will lead you past some of the park's most famous trees.

BEST VIEWS: Climb to the top of Moro Rock, high above the tall sequoia trees. On a clear day, you can see 100 miles (161 km) west.

BE EXTREME: Explore Crystal Cave, requiring a 15-minute hike down a steep path to the cave entrance.

ANIMAL SIGHTINGS: Bobcats, foxes, coyotes, squirrels, mule deer, frogs, beavers, turtles, and snakes. Black bears and mountain lions also call Sequoia home.

SHENANDOAH NATIONAL PARK

Virginia
Established December 26, 1935
197,411 acres (79,890 ha)
nps.gov/shen

RANGER TIPS
- Watch your footing on the slippery rocks around waterfalls.

- Avoid chasing and feeding the wildlife.
- Arrive early to avoid traffic jams on Skyline Drive.

TAKE IT EASY: Take a breather at the Dickey Ridge Picnic Area off Skyline Drive, a scenic spot within walking distance to hiking trails.

BEST VIEWS: Stop at Crescent Rock Overlook for a look at Hawksbill Mountain, the highest peak in the park. A challenging climb to the top of Bearfence Mountain rewards you with an awesome 360-degree view.

BE EXTREME: With an adult's supervision, take a dip in one of the park's many swimming holes, like the Hughes River in Nicholson Hollow.

ANIMAL SIGHTINGS: Opossums, gray foxes, bobcats, raccoons, black bears, white-tailed deer, salamanders, turtles, snakes, barred owls, red-tailed hawks, warblers, and woodpeckers

VIRGIN ISLANDS NATIONAL PARK

United States Virgin Islands
Established August 2, 1956
15,135 acres (6,125 ha)
nps.gov/viis

RANGER TIPS
- Wear water shoes while wading to avoid stepping on sharp shells and coral.
- Bring plenty of bug spray, sunscreen, water, and snacks.
- Visiting in the winter? Hit the Francis Bay Trail for spectacular bird-watching.

TAKE IT EASY: Wiggle your toes in the sands of the park's famous beaches, like Hawksnest Bay, Trunk Bay, and Cinnamon Bay.

BEST VIEWS: Hike to the end of the Ram Head Trail for a sweeping view of the Caribbean Sea from a height of 200 feet (61 m).

BE EXTREME: Snorkel along an underwater nature trail in Trunk Bay.

ANIMAL SIGHTINGS: Sea turtles, pelicans, frigatebirds, mongooses, and a rainbow of tropical fish

VOYAGEURS NATIONAL PARK

Minnesota
Established April 8, 1975
218,054 acres (88,243 ha)
nps.gov/voya

RANGER TIPS
- Always wear a life jacket when you're on the water. It's the law!
- Avoid attracting bears by keeping your food properly stored and carrying all of your garbage out of the park with you.
- Don't drink the lake water unless you filter it first.

TAKE IT EASY: Park your car by the Ash River Visitor Center, where you can relax in the shade before hiking to the Voyageurs Forest Overlook.

BEST VIEWS: Take a 2-mile (3.2-km) hike to the Anderson Bay Overlook, offering a cliff-top view of sparkling Rainy Lake.

BE EXTREME: In the summer, launch a kayak down any of the park's 45 miles (72.4 km) of water-accessible trails. In the winter, catch a ride on a snowmobile or explore the area on cross-country skis.

ANIMAL SIGHTINGS: Bald eagles, wolves, muskrats, loons, blue-winged teal, and beavers

WRANGELL-ST. ELIAS NATIONAL PARK AND PRESERVE

Alaska
Established December 2, 1980
13,188,000 acres (5,337,003 ha)
nps.gov/wrst

RANGER TIPS
- When to head to Wrangell-St. Elias? Think summer. June is best for wildflowers; July has the warmest days; berries ripen in August.
- Bring bug spray, a head net, and an insect-proof tent to protect against mosquitoes in the summer.
- On clear, cold days look for steam plumes rising from Mount Wrangell, an active volcano.

TAKE IT EASY: Stop at the McCarthy Lodge for a mouthwatering meal of fresh fish and locally grown produce or pack a picnic and spread it out at the Liberty Falls campground area.

BEST VIEWS: The windy, rocky McCarthy Road dead-ends at an eye-popping overlook of four rivers, lakes, forest, snowcapped mountains, and more.

BE EXTREME: Shoot the rapids of Copper River on a guided raft trip.

ANIMAL SIGHTINGS: Grizzly and black bears, moose, elk, bald eagles, game fish, sheep, caribou, goats, coyotes, red foxes, wolverines, and porcupines

⇔ Afterword

IF I ASKED YOU to close your eyes and imagine a classroom, what would you see? Chairs and desks? Walls and whiteboards? Most classrooms we think of are inside places, but what about outside places?

NatureBridge believes national parks are spectacular outdoor classrooms. Each one has the power to amaze us with the grandeur of the natural world. Taking in the majestic views of the Grand Canyon, spotting huge bison in Yellowstone, or hiking through the beautiful Golden Gate National Recreation Area, you are not just surrounded by awe-inspiring sights, you also have the opportunity to learn about the land, the people, and the wildlife that make our country so special.

Since 1971, NatureBridge and the National Park Service have partnered to inspire learning in our national parks. Imagine staying overnight in a national park with your classmates and teachers. You spend your days being fully absorbed in nature—smelling, touching, hearing, and, sometimes, even tasting the outdoors! Instead of reading about the science of the water cycle, you see it in person as you hike along a flowing river and search for hidden sources of water in the ground.

At NatureBridge, science takes place in living laboratories outside the confines of textbooks, and turns into important, real-world learning opportunities. The science you do in our national parks doesn't end in a test; it actually makes a difference in ensuring our national parks exist for the next hundred years!

Join us to experience the wonder and science of nature where students—like you—leave with a better understanding of our national parks, and a desire to protect them for generations. NatureBridge has brought more than one million students into the seven national parks where we lead programs: Yosemite, Golden Gate, Olympic, Santa Monica Mountains, Channel Islands, Shenandoah, and Prince William Forest National Park. Many other national parks have exciting programs, too!

As we enter the centennial of the National Park Service, NatureBridge hopes to bring one million more students to the great outdoors. Don't you think every young person should have the opportunity to learn in these beautiful places? We do, too!

Stephen Streufert
NatureBridge

⇢ National Park Properties by State or Territory

ALABAMA

- Horseshoe Bend National Military Park
- Little River Canyon National Preserve
- Russell Cave National Monument
- Tuskegee Airmen National Historic Site
- Tuskegee Institute National Historic Site

ALASKA

- Alagnak Wild River
- Aniakchak National Monument and Preserve
- Bering Land Bridge National Preserve
- Cape Krusenstern National Monument
- Klondike Gold Rush National Historical Park (a separate part of the park is in WA)
- Noatak National Preserve
- Sitka National Historical Park
- Yukon–Charley Rivers National Preserve

ARIZONA

- Canyon de Chelly National Monument
- Casa Grande Ruins National Monument
- Chiricahua National Monument
- Coronado National Memorial
- Fort Bowie National Historic Site
- Glen Canyon National Recreation Area (spans into UT)
- Grand Canyon–Parashant National Monument
- Hohokam Pima National Monument
- Hubbell Trading Post National Historic Site
- Lake Mead National Recreation Area (spans into NV)
- Montezuma Castle National Monument
- Navajo National Monument
- Organ Pipe Cactus National Monument
- Pipe Spring National Monument
- Sunset Crater Volcano National Monument
- Tonto National Monument
- Tumacácori National Historical Park
- Tuzigoot National Monument
- Walnut Canyon National Monument
- Wupatki National Monument

ARKANSAS

- Arkansas Post National Memorial

- Buffalo National River
- Fort Smith National Historic Site (spans into OK)
- Little Rock Central High School National Historic Site
- Pea Ridge National Military Park
- President William Jefferson Clinton Birthplace Home National Historic Site

CALIFORNIA

- Cabrillo National Monument
- César E. Chávez National Monument
- Devils Postpile National Monument
- Eugene O'Neill National Historic Site
- Fort Point National Historic Site
- Golden Gate National Recreation Area
- John Muir National Historic Site
- Lava Beds National Monument
- Manzanar National Historic Site
- Mojave National Preserve
- Muir Woods National Monument
- Pinnacles National Monument
- Point Reyes National Seashore
- Port Chicago Naval Magazine National Memorial
- Rosie the Riveter/World War II Home Front National Historical Park
- San Francisco Maritime National Historical Park
- Santa Monica Mountains National Recreation Area
- Whiskeytown National Recreation Area

COLORADO

- Bent's Old Fort National Historic Site
- Colorado National Monument
- Curecanti National Recreation Area
- Dinosaur National Monument (spans into UT)
- Florissant Fossil Beds National Monument
- Hovenweep National Monument (spans into UT)
- Sand Creek Massacre National Historic Site
- Yucca House National Monument

CONNECTICUT

- Weir Farm National Historic Site

DELAWARE

- First State National Historic Park (spans into PA)

163

DISTRICT OF COLUMBIA
- African American Civil War Memorial
- Carter G. Woodson Home National Historic Site
- Chesapeake & Ohio Canal National Historical Park (spans into MD, WV)
- Constitution Gardens
- George Mason Memorial
- Ford's Theatre National Historic Site
- Franklin Delano Roosevelt Memorial
- Frederick Douglass National Historic Site
- John Ericsson National Memorial
- Korean War Veterans Memorial
- Lincoln Memorial
- Lyndon Baines Johnson Memorial Grove-on-the-Potomac
- Martin Luther King, Jr., Memorial
- Mary McLeod Bethune Council House National Historic Site
- National Capital Parks-East (spans into MD)
- National Mall and Memorial Parks
- National World War II Memorial
- Pennsylvania Avenue National Historic Site
- President's Park (White House)
- Rock Creek Park
- Theodore Roosevelt Island National Memorial
- Thomas Jefferson Memorial
- Vietnam Veterans Memorial
- Washington Monument

FLORIDA
- Big Cypress National Preserve
- Canaveral National Seashore
- Castillo de San Marcos National Monument
- De Soto National Memorial
- Fort Caroline National Memorial
- Fort Matanzas National Monument
- Gulf Islands National Seashore (spans into MS)
- Timucuan Ecological and Historic Preserve

GEORGIA
- Andersonville National Cemetery
- Andersonville National Historic Site
- Chattahoochee River National Recreation Area
- Chickamauga and Chattanooga National Military Park (spans into TN)
- Cumberland Island National Seashore
- Fort Frederica National Monument
- Fort Pulaski National Monument
- Jimmy Carter National Historic Site
- Kennesaw Mountain National Battlefield Park
- Martin Luther King, Jr., National Historic Site
- Ocmulgee National Monument

GUAM
- War in the Pacific National Historical Park

HAWAII
- Kalaupapa National Historical Park
- Kaloko-Honokohau National Historical Park
- Pu'uhonua o Honaunau National Historical Park
- Pu'ukohola Heiau National Historic Site
- WWII Valor in the Pacific National Monument (spans into AK, CA)

IDAHO
- City of Rocks National Reserve
- Craters of the Moon National Monument and Preserve
- Hagerman Fossil Beds National Monument
- Minidoka National Historic Site
- Nez Perce National Historical Park (spans into MT, OR, WA)

ILLINOIS
- Lincoln Home National Historic Site

INDIANA
- George Rogers Clark National Historical Park
- Indiana Dunes National Lakeshore
- Lincoln Boyhood National Memorial

IOWA
- Effigy Mounds National Monument
- Herbert Hoover National Historic Site

KANSAS
- Brown v. Board of Education National Historic Site
- Fort Larned National Historic Site
- Fort Scott National Historic Site
- Nicodemus National Historic Site
- Tallgrass Prairie National Preserve

KENTUCKY
- Abraham Lincoln Birthplace National Historical Park
- Big South Fork National River and Recreation Area (spans into TN)
- Cumberland Gap National Historical Park (spans into TN, VA)

LOUISIANA
- Cane River Creole National Historical Park
- Chalmette National Cemetery
- Jean Lafitte National Historical Park and Preserve
- New Orleans Jazz National Historical Park
- Poverty Point National Monument

MAINE
- Maine Acadian Culture
- Roosevelt Campobello International Park
- Saint Croix Island International Historic Site

MARYLAND
- Antietam National Battlefield
- Antietam National Cemetery
- Assateague Island National Seashore (spans into VA)
- Catoctin Mountain Park
- Chesapeake & Ohio Canal National Historical Park (spans into DC, WV)
- Clara Barton National Historic Site
- Fort Foote Park
- Fort McHenry National Monument and Historic Shrine
- Fort Washington Park
- Glen Echo Park
- Greenbelt Park
- Hampton National Historic Site
- Harper's Ferry National Historic Park (spans into VA and WV)
- Harriet Tubman Underground Railroad National Monument
- Monocacy National Battlefield
- National Capital Park-East (spans into DC)
- Piscataway Park
- Thomas Stone National Historic Site

MASSACHUSETTS
- Adams National Historical Park
- Boston African American National Historic Site
- Boston Harbor Islands National Recreation Area
- Boston National Historical Park
- Cape Cod National Seashore
- Frederick Law Olmsted National Historic Site
- John Fitzgerald Kennedy National Historic Site
- Longfellow House—Washington's Headquarters National Historic Site
- Lowell National Historical Park
- Minute Man National Historical Park
- New Bedford Whaling National Historical Park
- Salem Maritime National Historic Site
- Saugus Iron Works National Historic Site
- Springfield Armory National Historic Site

MICHIGAN
- Keweenaw National Historical Park
- Pictured Rocks National Lakeshore
- River Raisin National Battlefield Park
- Sleeping Bear Dunes National Lakeshore

MINNESOTA
- Grand Portage National Monument
- Mississippi National River and Recreation Area
- Pipestone National Monument
- Saint Croix National Scenic Riverway (spans into WI)

MISSISSIPPI
- Brices Cross Roads National Battlefield
- Gulf Islands National Seashore (spans into FL)
- Natchez National Historical Park
- Natchez Trace Parkway
- Shiloh National Military Park
- Tupelo National Battlefield
- Vicksburg National Cemetery
- Vicksburg National Military Park (spans into LA)

MISSOURI
- George Washington Carver National Monument
- Harry S Truman National Historic Site
- Jefferson National Expansion Memorial
- Ozark National Scenic Riverways
- Ulysses S. Grant National Historic Site
- Wilson's Creek National Battlefield

MONTANA
- Big Hole National Battlefield
- Bighorn Canyon National Recreation Area (spans into WY)

165

- Custer National Cemetery
- Fort Union Trading Post National Historic Site (spans into ND)
- Grant-Kohrs Ranch National Historic Site
- Little Bighorn Battlefield National Monument
- Nez Perce National Historical Park (spans into ID, OR, WA)

NEBRASKA

- Agate Fossil Beds National Monument
- Homestead National Monument of America
- Missouri National Recreational River (spans into SD)
- Niobrara National Scenic River
- Scotts Bluff National Monument

NEVADA

- Lake Mead National Recreation Area (spans into AZ)

NEW HAMPSHIRE

- Saint-Gaudens National Historic Site

NEW JERSEY

- Delaware Water Gap National Recreation Area (spans into PA)
- Ellis Island (spans into NY)
- Gateway National Recreation Area (spans into NY)
- Great Egg Harbor Scenic and Recreational River
- Morristown National Historical Park
- Paterson Great Falls National Historic Park
- Statue of Liberty National Monument (spans into NY)
- Thomas Edison National Historical Park

NEW MEXICO

- Aztec Ruins National Monument
- Bandelier National Monument
- Capulin Volcano National Monument
- Chaco Culture National Historical Park
- El Malpais National Monument
- El Morro National Monument
- Fort Union National Monument
- Gila Cliff Dwellings National Monument
- Pecos National Historical Park
- Petroglyph National Monument
- Salinas Pueblo Missions National Monument
- White Sands National Monument

NEW YORK

- African Burial Ground National Monument
- Castle Clinton National Monument
- Eleanor Roosevelt National Historic Site
- Ellis Island (spans into NY)
- Federal Hall National Memorial
- Fire Island National Seashore
- Fort Stanwix National Monument
- Gateway National Recreation Area (spans into NJ)
- General Grant National Memorial
- Governors Island National Monument
- Hamilton Grange National Memorial
- Home of Franklin D. Roosevelt National Historic Site
- Lower East Side Tenement Museum National Historic Site
- Martin Van Buren National Historic Site
- Sagamore Hill National Historic Site
- Saint Paul's Church National Historic Site
- Saratoga National Historical Park
- Statue of Liberty National Monument (spans into NJ)
- Theodore Roosevelt Birthplace National Historic Site
- Theodore Roosevelt Inaugural National Historic Site
- Thomas Cole National Historic Site
- Upper Delaware Scenic and Recreational River (spans into PA)
- Vanderbilt Mansion National Historic Site
- Women's Rights National Historical Park

NORTH CAROLINA

- Blue Ridge Parkway
- Cape Hatteras National Seashore
- Cape Lookout National Seashore
- Carl Sandburg Home National Historic Site
- Fort Raleigh National Historic Site
- Guilford Courthouse National Military Park
- Moores Creek National Battlefield
- Wright Brothers National Memorial

NORTH DAKOTA

- Fort Union Trading Post National Historic Site (spans into MT)
- Knife River Indian Villages National Historic Site

OHIO

- Charles Young Buffalo Soldiers National Historic Monument

- Dayton Aviation Heritage National Historical Park
- David Berger National Memorial
- Fallen Timbers Battlefield and Fort Miamis National Historic Site
- First Ladies National Historic Site
- Hopewell Culture National Historical Park
- James A. Garfield National Historic Site
- Perry's Victory and International Peace Memorial
- William Howard Taft National Historic Site

OKLAHOMA

- Chickasaw National Recreation Area
- Fort Smith National Historic Site (spans into AR)
- Oklahoma City National Memorial
- Washita Battlefield National Historic Site

OREGON

- Fort Vancouver National Historic Site (spans into WA)
- John Day Fossil Beds National Monument
- Lewis and Clark National and State Historical Parks (spans into WA)
- Nez Perce National Historical Park (spans into ID, MT, WA)
- Oregon Caves National Monument and Preserve

PENNSYLVANIA

- Allegheny Portage Railroad National Historic Site
- Delaware Water Gap National Recreation Area (spans into NJ)
- Edgar Allan Poe National Historic Site
- Eisenhower National Historic Site
- Gloria Dei Church National Historic Site
- First State National Historic Park (spans into DE)
- Flight 93 National Memorial
- Fort Necessity National Battlefield
- Friendship Hill National Historic Site
- Gettysburg National Cemetery
- Gettysburg National Military Park
- Gloria Dei Church National Historic Site
- Hopewell Furnace National Historic Site
- Independence National Historical Park
- Johnstown Flood National Memorial
- Middle Delaware National Scenic River (spans into NJ)
- Steamtown National Historic Site
- Thaddeus Kosciuszko National Memorial
- Upper Delaware Scenic and Recreational River (spans into NY)
- Valley Forge National Historical Park

PUERTO RICO

- San Juan National Historic Site

RHODE ISLAND

- Roger Williams National Memorial
- Touro Synagogue National Historic Site

SOUTH CAROLINA

- Charles Pinckney National Historic Site
- Cowpens National Battlefield
- Fort Sumter National Monument
- Kings Mountain National Military Park
- Ninety Six National Historic Site

SOUTH DAKOTA

- Jewel Cave National Monument
- Minuteman Missile National Historic Site
- Missouri National Recreational River (spans into NE)
- Mount Rushmore National Memorial

TENNESSEE

- Andrew Johnson National Cemetery
- Andrew Johnson National Historic Site
- Big South Fork National River and Recreation Area (spans into KY)
- Chickamauga and Chattanooga National Military Park (spans into GA)
- Cumberland Gap National Historical Park (spans into KY, VA)
- Fort Donelson National Battlefield
- Fort Donelson National Cemetery
- Obed Wild and Scenic River
- Shiloh National Cemetery
- Shiloh National Military Park
- Stones River National Battlefield
- Stones River National Cemetery

TEXAS

- Alibates Flint Quarries National Monument
- Amistad National Recreation Area
- Big Thicket National Preserve

167

- Chamizal National Memorial
- Fort Davis National Historic Site
- Lake Meredith National Recreation Area
- Lyndon B. Johnson National Historical Park
- Padre Island National Seashore
- Palo Alto Battlefield National Historical Park
- Rio Grande Wild and Scenic River
- San Antonio Missions National Historical Park

U.S. VIRGIN ISLANDS

- Buck Island Reef National Monument
- Christiansted National Historic Site
- Salt River Bay National Historical Park and Ecological Preserve
- Virgin Islands Coral Reef National Monument

UTAH

- Cedar Breaks National Monument
- Dinosaur National Monument (spans into CO)
- Glen Canyon National Recreation Area (spans into AZ)
- Golden Spike National Historic Site
- Hovenweep National Monument (spans into CO)
- Natural Bridges National Monument
- Rainbow Bridge National Monument
- Timpanogos Cave National Monument

VERMONT

- Marsh-Billings-Rockefeller National Historical Park

VIRGINIA

- Appomattox Court House National Historical Park
- Arlington House, The Robert E. Lee Memorial
- Arlington National Cemetery
- Assateague Island National Seashore (spans into MD)
- Blue Ridge Parkway
- Booker T. Washington National Monument
- Cedar Creek and Belle Grove National Historical Park
- Colonial National Historical Park
- Cumberland Gap National Historical Park (spans into KY, TN)
- Fort Monroe National Monument
- Fredericksburg National Cemetery
- Fredericksburg and Spotsylvania County Battlefields Memorial National Military Park
- George Washington Birthplace National Monument
- George Washington Memorial Parkway
- Harpers Ferry National Historic Park
- Maggie L. Walker National Historic Site
- Malvern Hill, Richmond National Battlefield Park
- Manassas National Battlefield Park
- Petersburg National Battlefield
- Poplar Grove National Cemetery
- Prince William Forest Park
- Richmond National Battlefield Park
- Wolf Trap National Park for the Performing Arts
- Yorktown National Cemetery

WASHINGTON

- Ebey's Landing National Historical Reserve
- Fort Vancouver National Historic Site (spans into OR)
- Klondike Gold Rush National Historical Park (spans into AK)
- Lake Chelan National Recreation Area
- Lake Roosevelt National Recreation Area
- Lewis and Clark National and State Historical Parks (spans into OR)
- Minidoka National Historic Site
- Nez Perce National Historical Park (spans into ID, MT, OR)
- Ross Lake National Recreation Area
- San Juan Islands National Historical Park
- Whitman Mission National Historic Site

WEST VIRGINIA

- Bluestone National Scenic River
- Chesapeake & Ohio Canal National Historical Park (spans into DC, MD)
- Gauley River National Recreation Area
- Harpers Ferry National Historical Park
- New River Gorge National River

WISCONSIN

- Apostle Islands National Lakeshore
- Saint Croix National Scenic Riverway (spans into MN)

WYOMING

- Bighorn Canyon National Recreation Area (spans into MT)

- Devils Tower National Monument
- Fort Butte National Monument
- Fort Laramie National Historic Site
- Fossil Butte National Monument
- John D. Rockefeller, Jr. Memorial Parkway

⇨ National Trails

- Ala Kahakai National Historic Trail (HI)
- Appalachian Trail (ME to GA)
- Arizona National Scenic Trail (AZ)
- California National Historic Trail (MO to CA)
- Captain John Smith Chesapeake National Historic Trail (DE to DC to MD to VA)
- Continental Divide National Scenic Trail (MT to NM)
- El Camino Real de los Tejas National Historic Trail (LA to TX)
- El Camino Real de Tierra Adentro National Historic Trail (NM)
- Florida National Scenic Trail (FL)
- Ice Age National Scenic Trail (WI)
- Iditarod National Historic Trail (AK)
- Juan Bautista de Anza National Historic Trail (AZ to CA)
- Lewis and Clark National Historic Trail (MO to OR)
- Mormon Pioneer National Historic Trail (MO to UT)
- Natchez Trace Trail (MS to TN)
- New England National Scenic Trail (CT to MA)
- New Jersey Coastal Heritage Trail (NJ)
- Nez Perce (Nee-Me-Poo) National Historic Trail (OR to MT)
- North Country National Scenic Trail (NY to ND)
- Old Spanish National Historic Trail (NM to CA)
- Oregon National Historic Trail (MO to OR)
- Overmountain Victory National Historic Trail (VA to TN to NC to SC)
- Pacific Crest National Scenic Trail (CA to WA)
- Pacific Northwest National Scenic Trail (MT to WA)
- Pony Express National Historic Trail (MO to CA)
- Potomac Heritage National Scenic Trail (VA to MD to PA to DC)

- Santa Fe National Historic Trail (MO to NM)
- Selma to Montgomery National Historic Trail (AL)
- Star-Spangled Banner National Historic Trail (DC to MD to VA)
- Trail of Tears National Historic Trail (TN to OK)
- Washington-Rochambeau Revolutionary Route National Historic Trail (MA to VA)

Glossary

archaeology: The science that deals with past human life and culture through the recovery of material remains, such as artifacts

artifact: An object or tool created by humans

biodiversity: The number of different species of plants and animals that live in a specific environment

canyon: A deep, narrow valley with steep sides

cave: A natural underground chamber that opens to the Earth's surface

cliff: A very steep rock face, usually along a coast but also on the side of a mountain

climate: Average weather conditions of a region

crater: A bowl-shaped hole in the Earth's surface caused by an explosion or the impact of another object

culture: The entire way of life shared by a group of people, including customs and beliefs

ecology: The science that deals with the relationship between living things and their environment

ecosystem: A system of living things that live together and interact with their environment

endangered: Plants or animals that are in danger of no longer being found in the wild because of loss of habitat or danger from humans

extinct: Plants or animals that have died out and no longer live on Earth

fossil: Preserved remains or traces of ancient plants and animals

geology: The study of the physical history of the Earth, its composition, its structure, and the processes that form and change it

geyser: A hot spring through which jets of water and steam erupt

glacier: A large, slow-moving mass of ice that forms over time from snow

gorge: A deep, narrow valley that has steep sides and is usually smaller than a canyon

grassland: Land covered in grasses instead of shrubs and trees; a prairie is a type of grassland

habitat: Natural home of a plant or animal

historical site: A structure or location where a special event or activity in history took place

landmark: An object or structure that marks a specific location or point of interest; a natural landmark is formed by forces in nature

landscape: Part of the Earth's surface that can be viewed at one time from one place

national park: An area of land set aside and protected by the government to preserve the special features within it

naturalist: A specialist who studies living things in nature

observation tower: A structure that

allows for a full and clear view of a landscape

paleontology: The science that deals with past living things through the recovery and study of fossils

panoramic: A complete view of a landscape in every direction

permit: A written form of permission to do something, like camp at a special spot or fish in a certain stream

precipitation: All of the forms in which water falls to the ground from the atmosphere, including rain and snow

ranger: A person who is in charge of helping protect and maintain special land, such as a national park

refuge: A place that provides protection for animals, especially endangered ones

sand dune: A mound of sand piled up by the wind

species: A group of plants or animals that share common characteristics

summit: The highest point, like the peak of a mountain

terrain: The surface features of land

topography: On a map, the illustration of features such as heights and depths

wetland: Land that is either covered or soaked by water, such as swamps, for at least part of the year

wildlife: Plants and animals that are found in nature

woodland: Land covered with trees and shrubs

Find Out More

A note for parents and teachers: For more information on this topic, you can visit these websites with your young readers.

For the online Junior Ranger Program visit: **nps.gov/kids/become-a-junior-ranger.htm**

You'll find even more fun with the National Park Service Kids website: **nps.gov/kids**

For more about the National Park Foundation: **nationalparks.org**

To learn about park geology and ecology visit the U.S. Geological Survey: **usgs.gov/geology-and-ecology-of-national-parks**

For games and great animal information visit: **natgeokids.com**

To learn more about Buddy Bison and the National Park Trust visit: **parktrust.org/overview/buddy-bison-school-program** and **parktrust.org**

Index

A
Acadia National Park, ME 16–19
Agate Fossil Beds National Monument, NE 62
Ala Kahakai National Historic Trail, HI 146
Alabama: national park properties 163
Alaska
    Denali National Park and Preserve 92–95, 144
    Gates of the Arctic National Park and Preserve 155
    Glacier Bay National Park and Preserve 155
    Katmai National Park and Preserve 156–157
    Kenai Fjords National Park 157
    Klondike Gold Rush National Historical Park 148
    Kobuk Valley National Park 157–158
    Lake Clark National Park and Preserve 158
    Mount McKinley 144
    national park properties 163
    World War II Valor in the Pacific National Monument 149
    Wrangell-St. Elias National Park and Preserve 162
Alcatraz Island, Golden Gate National Recreation Area, CA 81
American Samoa, National Park of 150–151, 152
Amistad National Recreation Area, TX 82
Apostle Islands National Lakeshore, WI 62
Arches National Park, UT 152
Arizona
    Canyon de Chelly National Monument 82
    Chiricahua National Monument 82
    Glen Canyon National Recreation Area 83
    Grand Canyon National Park 76–79
    Lake Mead National Recreation Area 148
    national park properties 163
    Petrified Forest National Park 123
    Saguaro National Park 160
Arkansas
    Hot Springs National Park 30–33
    national park properties 163
Assateague Island National Seashore, MD-VA 26

B
Badlands National Park, SD 42–45
Bandelier National Monument, NM 82
Big Bend National Park, TX 68–71
Big Thicket National Preserve, TX 82
Bighorn Canyon National Recreation Area, MT-WY 146
Biscayne National Park, FL 152
Black Canyon of the Gunnison National Park, CO 152–153
Boston National Historical Park, MA 34
Bryce Canyon National Park, UT 88–91

C
Cabrillo National Monument, CA 146
California
    Alcatraz Island, Golden Gate National Recreation Area 81
    Cabrillo National Monument 146
    Channel Islands National Park 154
    Death Valley National Park 81, 144
    Golden Gate National Recreation Area 147
    Joshua Tree National Park 114–117
    Kings Canyon National Park 157
    Lassen Volcanic National Park 158
    Muir Woods National Monument 148
    national park properties 163
    Redwood National Park 145
    Santa Monica Mountains National Recreation Area 149
    Sequoia National Park 145, 160
    World War II Valor in the Pacific National Monument 149
    Yosemite National Park 25, 84–85, 136–139
Canyon de Chelly National Monument, AZ 82
Canyonlands National Park, UT 153
Cape Cod National Seashore, MA 36
Capitol Reef National Park, UT 153
Captain John Smith Chesapeake National Historic Trail 36
Carlsbad Caverns National Park, NM 64–65, 72–75
Cedar Breaks National Monument,
UT 146
Chaco Culture National Historical Park, NM 82
Channel Islands National Park, CA 154
Chiricahua National Monument, AZ 82
Clark, Lake, AK 158
Colonial National Historical Park, VA 36
Colorado
    Black Canyon of the Gunnison National Park 152–153
    Colorado National Monument 146
    Dinosaur National Monument 123, 147
    Great Sand Dunes National Park 81
    Hovenweep National Monument 147–148
    Mesa Verde National Park 159
    national park properties 163
    Rocky Mountain National Park 128–131
    Santa Fe National Historic Trail 83
Colorado National Monument, CO 146
Congaree National Park, SC 154
Connecticut: national park properties 163
Crater Lake National Park, OR 25
Craters of the Moon National Monument and Preserve, ID 146
Cuyahoga Valley National Park, OH 46–49

D
Death Valley National Park, CA-NV 81, 144
Delaware
    Captain John Smith Chesapeake National Historic Trail 36
    national park properties 163
Delaware Water Gap National Recreation Area, NJ-PA 36
Denali National Park and Preserve, AK 92–95, 144
Devils Tower National Monument, WY 81, 147
Dinosaur National Monument, CO-UT 123, 147
District of Columbia
    Captain John Smith Chesapeake National Historic Trail 36
    National Mall and Memorial Parks 35
national park properties 164
Theodore Roosevelt Island 25
Dry Tortugas National Park, FL 154–155

E
Ellis Island, NJ-NY 34
Endangered species 100–101
Everglades National Park, FL 12–13, 20–23

F
Florida
    Biscayne National Park 152
    Dry Tortugas National Park 154–155
    Everglades National Park 12–13, 20–23
    Gulf Islands National Seashore 37
    national park properties 164
Fort Sumter National Monument, SC 36
Fort Vancouver National Historic Site, OR-WA 147
Fossil Butte National Monument, WY 123, 147
Fossils 122–123

G
Gates of the Arctic National Park and Preserve, AK 155
Georgia
    Kennesaw Mountain National Battlefield Park 37
    national park properties 164
Gila Cliff Dwellings National Monument, NM 83
Glacier Bay National Park and Preserve, AK 155
Glacier National Park, MT 96–99
Glen Canyon National Recreation Area, AZ-UT 83
Glossary 170–171
Golden Gate National Recreation Area, CA 147
Grand Canyon National Park, AZ 76–79
Grand Teton National Park, WY 102–105
Great Basin National Park, NV 155–156
Great Sand Dunes National Park, CO 81
Great Smoky Mountains National Park, NC-TN 26–29, 145
Guadalupe Mountains National Park, TX 156
Guam
    national park properties 164
    War in the Pacific National Historical Park 149

172

Index

Gulf Islands National Seashore, FL-MS 37

H
Haleakalā National Park, HI 106–109
Harriet Tubman Underground Railroad National Monument, MD 37
Hawaii
   Ala Kahakai National Historic Trail 146
   Haleakalā National Park 106–109
   Hawai'i Volcanoes National Park 110–113
   national park properties 164
   Pu'uhonua o Hōnaunau National Historical Park 149
   World War II Valor in the Pacific National Monument 149
Hawai'i Volcanoes National Park, HI 110–113
Hot Springs National Park, AR 30–33
Hovenweep National Monument, CO-UT 147–148

I
Ice Age National Scenic Trail, WI 62
Idaho
   Craters of the Moon National Monument and Preserve 146
   Lewis & Clark National Historic Trail 62
   national park properties 164
   Yellowstone National Park 132–135
Illinois
   Jefferson National Expansion Memorial 62
   Lewis & Clark National Historic Trail 62
   national park properties 164
Indiana: national park properties 164
Iowa
   Lewis & Clark National Historic Trail 62
   national park properties 164
Isle Royale National Park, MI 156

J
Jefferson National Expansion Memorial, IL-MO 62
Joshua Tree National Park, CA 114–117

K
Kansas
   Lewis & Clark National Historic Trail 62
   national park properties 164
   Santa Fe National Historic Trail 83
   Tallgrass Prairie National Preserve 63
Katmai National Park and Preserve, AK 156–157
Kenai Fjords National Park, AK 157
Kennesaw Mountain National Battlefield Park, GA 37
Kentucky
   Mammoth Cave National Park 144, 158–159
   national park properties 165
Kings Canyon National Park, CA 157
Klondike Gold Rush National Historical Park, AK-WA 148
Kobuk Valley National Park, AK 157–158

L
Lake Clark National Park and Preserve, AK 158
Lake Mead National Recreation Area, AZ-NV 148
Lake Meredith National Recreation Area, TX 83
Lake Roosevelt National Recreation Area, WA 148
Lassen Volcanic National Park, CA 158
Lewis & Clark National Historic Trail 62
Little Bighorn Battlefield National Monument, MT 35, 148
Louisiana: national park properties 165

M
Maine
   Acadia National Park 16–19
   national park properties 165
Mammoth Cave National Park, KY 144, 158–159
Map 10–11
Map key 9
Maryland
   Assateague Island National Seashore 36
   Captain John Smith Chesapeake National Historic Trail 36
   Harriet Tubman Underground Railroad National Monument 37
   national park properties 165
Massachusetts
   Boston National Historical Park 34
   Cape Cod National Seashore 36
   national park properties 165
   Salem Maritime National Historic Site 37
McKinley, Mount, AK 92–95, 144
Mead, Lake, AZ-NV 150
Meredith, Lake, TX 83
Mesa Verde National Park, CO 159
Michigan
   Isle Royale National Park 156
   national park properties 165
   Pictured Rocks National Lakeshore 63
   Sleeping Bear Dunes National Lakeshore 63
Minnesota
   Mississippi National River and Recreation Area 62–63
   national park properties 165
   Voyageurs National Park 161
Mississippi
   Gulf Islands National Seashore 37
   national park properties 165
Mississippi National River and Recreation Area, MN 62–63
Missouri
   Jefferson National Expansion Memorial 62
   Lewis & Clark National Historic Trail 62
   national park properties 165
   Ozark National Scenic Riverways National River 63
   Santa Fe National Historic Trail 83
Montana
   Bighorn Canyon National Recreation Area 146
   Glacier National Park 96–99
   Lewis & Clark National Historic Trail 62
   Little Bighorn Battlefield National Monument 35, 148
   national park properties 165–166
   Yellowstone National Park 132–135
Mount Desert Island, ME 16–19
Mount McKinley, AK 144
Mount Rainier National Park, WA 118–121
Mount Rushmore National Memorial, SD 45, 63
Muir Woods National Monument, CA 148

N
National Mall and Memorial Parks, DC 35
National Park of American Samoa, AS 150–151, 152
National trails 169
Nebraska
   Agate Fossil Beds National Monument 62
   Lewis & Clark National Historic Trail 62
   national park properties 166
Nevada
   Death Valley National Park 144
   Great Basin National Park 155–156
   Lake Mead National Recreation Area 148
   national park properties 166
New Hampshire: national park properties 166
New Jersey
   Delaware Water Gap National Recreation Area 36
   national park properties 166
   Paterson Great Falls National Historical Park 37
   Statue of Liberty & Ellis Island 34
New Mexico
   Bandelier National Monument 82
   Carlsbad Caverns National Park 64–65, 72–75
   Chaco Culture National Historical Park 82
   Gila Cliff Dwellings National Monument 83
   national park properties 166
   Petroglyph National Monument 83
   Santa Fe National Historic Trail 83
New York
   Captain John Smith Chesapeake National Historic Trail 36
   national park properties 166
   Statue of Liberty & Ellis Island 34
   Theodore Roosevelt Birthplace National Historic Site 25
North Carolina
   Great Smoky Mountains National Park 26–29, 145
   national park properties 166
   Wright Brothers National Memorial 37
North Cascades National Park, WA 159

Index

North Dakota
    Lewis & Clark National Historic Trail 62
    national park properties 166
    Theodore Roosevelt National Park 38–39, 52–55
    Wind Cave National Park 56–59

O
Ohio
    Cuyahoga Valley National Park 46–49
    national park properties 166–167
Oklahoma
    national park properties 167
    Santa Fe National Historic Trail 83
Olympic National Park, WA 124–127
Oregon
    Crater Lake National Park 25
    Fort Vancouver National Historic Site 147
    Lewis & Clark National Historic Trail 62
    national park properties 167
    Oregon Caves National Monument 148
Oregon Caves National Monument, OR 148
Ozark National Scenic Riverways National River, MO 63

P
Packing your suitcase 50–51
Padre Island National Seashore, TX 83
Paterson Great Falls National Historical Park, NJ 37
Pennsylvania
    Captain John Smith Chesapeake National Historic Trail 36
    Delaware Water Gap National Recreation Area 36
    national park properties 167
Petrified Forest National Park, AZ 123
Petroglyph National Monument, NM 83
Pictured Rocks National Lakeshore, MI 63
Puerto Rico: national park properties 167
Puʻuhonua o Hōnaunau National Historical Park, HI 149

R
Rainbow Bridge National Monument, UT 145
Rainier, Mount, WA 118–121
Record-setting parks 144–145
Redwood National Park, CA 145

Rhode Island: national park properties 167
Rocky Mountain National Park, CO 128–131
Roosevelt, Lake, WA 148
Roosevelt, Theodore "Teddy" 24–25

S
Saguaro National Park, AZ 160
Salem Maritime National Historic Site, MA 37
San Juan Island National Historical Park, WA 149
Santa Fe National Historic Trail 83
Santa Monica Mountains National Recreation Area, CA 149
Sequoia National Park, CA 145, 160
Shenandoah National Park, VA 160–161
Sleeping Bear Dunes National Lakeshore, MI 63
South Carolina
    Congaree National Park 154
    Fort Sumter National Monument 36
    national park properties 167
South Dakota
    Badlands National Park 42–45
    Lewis & Clark National Historic Trail 62
    Mount Rushmore National Memorial 45, 63
    national park properties 167
Spooky sites 80–81
Statue of Liberty & Ellis Island, NJ-NY 34

T
Tallgrass Prairie National Preserve, KS 63
Tennessee
    Great Smoky Mountains National Park 26–29, 145
    national park properties 167
Texas
    Amistad National Recreation Area 82
    Big Bend National Park 68–71
    Big Thicket National Preserve 82
    Guadalupe Mountains National Park 156
    Lake Meredith National Recreation Area 83
    national park properties 167–168
    Padre Island National Seashore 83
Theodore Roosevelt Birthplace National Historic Site, NY 25

Theodore Roosevelt Island, DC 25
Theodore Roosevelt National Park, ND 38–39, 52–55

U
U.S. Virgin Islands
    national park properties 168
    Virgin Islands National Park 161
Utah
    Arches National Park 152
    Bryce Canyon National Park 88–91
    Canyonlands National Park 153
    Capitol Reef National Park 153
    Cedar Breaks National Monument 146
    Dinosaur National Monument 123, 147
    Glen Canyon National Recreation Area 83
    Hovenweep National Monument 147–148
    national park properties 168
    Rainbow Bridge National Monument 145
    Zion National Park 140–143

V
Vermont: national park properties 168
Virgin Islands
    national park properties 168
    Virgin Islands National Park 161
Virgin Islands National Park, VI 161
Virginia
    Assateague Island National Seashore 36
    Captain John Smith Chesapeake National Historic Trail 36
    Colonial National Historical Park 36
    national park properties 168
    Shenandoah National Park 160–161
Voyageurs National Park, MN 161

W
War in the Pacific National Historical Park, GU 149
Washington
    Fort Vancouver National Historic Site 147
    Klondike Gold Rush National Historical Park 148
    Lake Roosevelt National Recreation Area 148
    Lewis & Clark National Historic Trail 62

Mount Rainier National Park 118–121
    national park properties 168
    North Cascades National Park 159
    Olympic National Park 124–127
    San Juan Island National Historical Park 149
Washington, D.C.
    Captain John Smith Chesapeake National Historic Trail 36
    National Mall and Memorial Parks 35
    national park properties 164
    Theodore Roosevelt Island 25
West Virginia: national park properties 168
Wildlife 60–61, 100–101
Wind Cave National Park, ND 56–59
Wisconsin
    Apostle Islands National Lakeshore 62
    Ice Age National Scenic Trail 62
    national park properties 168
World War II Valor in the Pacific National Monument 149
Wrangell-St. Elias National Park and Preserve, AK 162
Wright Brothers National Memorial, NC 37
Wyoming
    Bighorn Canyon National Recreation Area 146
    Devils Tower National Monument 81, 147
    Fossil Butte National Monument 123, 147
    Grand Teton National Park 102–105
    national park properties 168–169
    Yellowstone National Park 132–135

Y
Yellowstone National Park 132–135
Yosemite National Park, CA 25, 84–85, 136–139

Z
Zion National Park, UT 140–143

Photo Credits

NGIC=National Geographic Image Collection; AL=Alamy Stock Photo; CO=Corbis; GI=Getty Images; MP=Minden Pictures; SS=Shutterstock

Front Cover: (grizzly bear in Katmai National Park), Andy Rouse/Nature Picture Library; (Martin Luther King, Jr. Memorial in Washington, D.C.), Grant Faint/Photo-library RM/GI; (kayaking in Grand Teton National Park), Jeff Diener/Aurora Creative/GI; (Arches National Park), Photodisc; **Back Cover:** (condor), Momatiuk - Eastcott/CO; (ram), Bryan Peterson/The Image Bank/GI; (trail ride), Richard Nowitz/NGIC; (lighthouse), Ocean/CO; (canoe), MountainHardcore/SS; **Spine,** Jose Azel/Aurora Creative/GI; **Front Matter:** 2-3, Roger Ressmeyer/CO; 4 (LO LE), Jim Sugar/CO; 4 (LO RT), Joe Klementovich/Aurora Open/GI; 5 (UP LE), Steven Kazlowski/Science Faction/GI; 5 (UP RT), Reinhard Dirscherl/Visuals Unlimited, Inc.; 6, Norbert Rosing/NGIC; 7 (UP LE), Katrina Leigh/SS; 7 (UP CTR LE), Lake County Museum/CO; 7 (UP RT), Heath Korvola/Lifesize/GI; 7 (UP CTR RT), John & Lisa Merrill/Photodisc/GI; 7 (CTR CTR), Michael Melford/NGIC; 7 (CTR RT), Tom Brakefield/Brand X/GI; 7 (CTR LE), Harry Thomas/iStockphoto; 7 (LO LE), Rough Guides/Paul Whitfield/Axiom RM/GI; 7 (CTR CTR), Bill Hatcher/NGIC; 7 (LO RT), pmphoto/SS; 7 (LO RT), Dean Conger/NGIC; 8 (UP), John Eastcott and Yva Momatiuk/NGIC; 8 (CTR LE), Supri Suharjoto/SS; 8 (LO LE), Matthijs Wetterauw/SS; 8 (UP RT), Dick Durrance II/NGIC; 8 (LO RT), mlorenz/SS; **THE EAST:** 12-13, Daniel J. Cox/Photographer's Choice/GI; 16 (UP), Atlantide Phototravel/CO; 16 (LO), Scott Smith/CO/CO; 17 (UP), Michael Melford/NGIC; 17 (LE CTR), Jose Azel/Aurora Creative/GI; 17 (RT CTR), Nicolaus Czarnecki/Zuma Press; 17 (LO), Michael Melford/NGIC; 18-19 (BACK), Roman Sigaev/SS; 18 (UP), Nicolaus Czarnecki/Zuma Press/CO; 18 (LO), Warren Marr/Panoramic Images/NGIC; 19 (UP), Ocean/CO; 19 (CTR), Raymond Gehman/NGIC; 19 (LO), Danita Delimont/AL; 20 (UP), Richard T. Nowitz/NGIC; 20 (LO), Visuals Unlimited/CO; 21 (UP), Walter Bibikow/CO; 21 (CTR), Silken Photography/SS; 21 (LO LE), Richard T. Nowitz/GI; 21 (LO RT), Michael Patrick O'Neill/AL; 22-23 (BACK), Roman Sigaev/SS; 22 (UP), Tim Laman/NGIC; 22 (LO), Mike Theiss/NGIC; 23 (UP), Rich Reid/NGIC; 23 (CTR), Marilyn Angel Wynn/Nativestock/GI; 23 (LO), Patrick Ward/CO; 24 (UP), Tom Murphy/NGIC; 24 (CTR), Underwood Archives/The Image Works; 24 (LO), vdbvsl/AL; 25 (UP), Lonely Planet/GI; 25 (CTR RT), compassandcamera/iStockphoto; 25 (CTR LE), Gerry Ellis/MP; 25 (LO CTR), Chuck Myers/Zuma Press/CO; 26 (UP), Bob Pool/GI; 26 (LO), Raymond Gehman/CO; 27 (UP), Carr Clifton/MP; 27 (CTR), Michael Runkel/Robert Harding World Imagery/GI; 27 (LO LE), Tim Fitzharriz/MP/NGIC; 27 (LO RT), Raymond Gehman/NGIC; 28-29 (BACK), Roman Sigaev/SS; 28 (UP), Corey Nolen/Aurora Open/GI; 28 (LO LE), Amy White & Al Petteway/NGIC; 28 (LO RT), Ocean/CO; 29 (UP), Purestock/GI; 29 (LO), Tom Nebbia/CO; 30 (UP), Jay Sabo/AL; 30 (LO), Lake County Museum/CO; 31 (UP CTR), Michael Snell/AL; 31 (UP RT), Kelly Shipp/AL; 31 (LO LE), Jeff Greenberg/AL; 31 (LO RT), Buddy Mays/AL; 32-33 (BACK), Roman Sigaev/SS; 32 (UP), kaband/SS; 32 (CTR), Buddy Mays/CO; 32 (LO), Declan Haun/NGIC; 33 (CTR), Matt Bradley/NGIC; 33 (LO), Terry Smith Images Arkansas Picture Library/AL; 34 (UP), Joseph Sohm/CO; 34 (CTR), iofoto/SS; 34 (LO), Marcio Silva/Dreamstime; 35 (UP), imagebroker/AL; 35 (CTR), B Christopher/AL; 35 (LO LE), Coloradonative/Dreamstime; 35 (LO RT), Jruffa/Dreamstime; **THE MIDWEST:** 38-39, Steve Kaufman/CO; 42 (UP), Flickr RM/GI; 42 (LO), F. Barbagallo/DEA/GI; 43 (UP), Carr Clifton/MP/NGIC; 43 (CTR), Patrick Chatelain/Radius Images/CO; 43 (LO LE), Layne Kennedy/CO; 43 (LO RT), Layne Kennedy/CO; 44-45 (BACK), Roman Sigaev/SS; 44 (UP), Danita Delimont/AL; 44 (CTR), Carr Clifton/MP/NGIC; 44 (LO), Connie Ricca/CO; 45 (UP), Jim Brandenburg/MP/NGIC; 45 (LO), Mike Nelson/EP/CO; 46 (UP), Kenneth Sponsler/AL; 46 (LO), Danita Delimont/AL; 47 (UP), Jason Langley/AL; 47 (CTR), Jason Langley/AL; 47 (LO LE), Tom Uhlman/AL; 47 (LO RT), Joe McDonald/CO; 48-49 (BACK), Roman Sigaev/SS; 48 (UP), Kenneth Sponsler/AL; 48 (CTR), Stan Rohrer/AL; 48 (LO), Tom Uhlman/AL; 49 (UP), Tom Uhlman/AL; 49 (LO), Jeff Hackett/AL; 50 (UP LE), Steve Cukrov/SS; 50 (UP RT), DeiMosz/SS; 50 (CTR RT), Smiltena/SS; 50 (LO LE), chungking/SS; 50 (LO RT), pegasusa012/SS; 51 (UP), Dudarev Mikhail/SS; 51 (CTR LE), Arno Jenkins/SS; 51 (CTR RT), 2xSamara/SS; 51 (LO LE), Gustav Verderber/Visuals Unlimited/CO; 51 (LO RT), Gavran333/SS; 52 (UP), Michael Melford/NGIC; 52 (LO), Richard Cummins/CO; 53 (UP RT), Macduff Everton/CO; 53 (UP LE), Phil Schermeister/NGIC; 53 (LO LE), Tim Fitzharris/MP; 53 (LO RT), Farrell Grehan/NGIC; 54-55 (BACK), Roman Sigaev/SS; 54 (UP), Richard Cummins/CO; 54 (CTR), Connie Ricca/CO; 54 (LO), Michele Falzone/JAI/CO; 55 (UP), Tim Fitzharris/CO; 55 (LO), Tom Bean/CO; 56 (UP), Robert E. Barber/AL; 56 (LO), Blaine Harrington III/CO; 57 (UP), Patrick Chatelain/CO; 57 (CTR), Michelle Gilders/AL; 57 (LO LE), Bobby Model/NGIC/GI; 57 (LO RT), Michelle Gilders/AL; 58-59 (BACK), Roman Sigaev/SS; 58 (UP), James Hager/Robert Harding World Imagery/CO; 58 (LO LE), Blaine Harrington III/CO; 58 (LO RT), James Metcalf/iStockphoto; 59 (UP), Bobby Model/NGIC; 59 (LO), Patrick Chatelain/CO; 60 (UP LE), Ekaterina Pokrovsky/Dreamstime; 60 (UP RT), Danita Delimon/GI; 60 (LO), All Canada Photos/AL; 61 (UP LE), Michael Patrick O'Neill/AL; 61 (UP RT), Chris Hill/SS; 61 (CTR), Dr. P. Marazzi/Science Source; 61 (LO LE), Design Pics Inc/AL; 61 (LO RT), Thomas & Pat Leeson/Science Source; **THE SOUTHWEST:** 64-65, Adam Woolfitt/CO; 68 (UP), Rusty Dodson/SS; 68 (LO), Whit Richardson/AL; 69 (UP), Ian Shive/Aurora Photos; 69 (CTR), Cheah Chin-Hong/SS; 69 (LO LE), Buddy Mays/AL; 69 (LO RT), Rich Reid/NGIC; 70-71 (BACK), Roman Sigaev/SS; 70 (UP), Whit Richardson/AL; 70 (LO), David Nevala/GI; 71 (UP), Tim Fitzharris/MP; 71 (CTR), fotum/SS; 71 (LO), Bobbie DeHerrera/Newsmakers/GI; 72 (UP), Rich Reid/NGIC; 72 (LO), Stephen St. John/NGIC; 73 (UP), Walter Meayers Edwards/NGIC; 73 (CTR), John Cancalosi/Photolibrary; 73 (LO LE), Michael Nichols/NGIC; 73 (LO RT), Ameng Wu/iStockphoto; 74-75 (BACK), Roman Sigaev/SS; 74 (UP RT), Panoramic Images/GI; 74 (CTR LE), Michael Nichols/NGIC; 74 (LO), Michael Durham; 75 (UP), JTB Photo Communications, Inc./AL; 75 (LO), Michael Nichols/NGIC; 76 (UP), Tim Fitzharris/MP/NGIC; 76 (LO), John Burcham/NGIC; 77 (UP RT), Michael DeYoung/CO; 77 (UP LE), Jenny E. Ross/CO; 77 (LO LE), Tom Bean/AL; 77 (LO RT), Momatiuk - Eastcott/CO; 78-79, Roman SIgaev/SS; 78 (UP RT), nobleIMAGES/AL; 78 (UP LE), Russ Bishop/AL; 78 (LO), David Kadlubowski/CO; 79 (UP), lucky-photographer/iStockphoto; 79 (LO), Craig MacDonnell/SS; 80 (UP), f11photo/SS; 80 (CTR), Jim West/AL; 80 (LO), Michael Couron/Dreamstime; 81 (UP LE), Naaman Abreu/SS; 81 (UP RT), Hulton Archive/GI; 81 (CTR), Pegaz/AL; 81 (LO LE), GUIZIOU Franck/CO; 81 (LO RT), Gary Hartz/Dreamstime; **THE WEST:** 84-85, Bill Ross/CO; 88 (UP), Raul Touzon/NGIC; 88 (LO), George F. Mobley/NGIC; 89 (UP), Tim Fitzharris/MP/NGIC; 89 (CTR), Scott T. Smith/CO; 89 (LO LE), George H.H. Huey/CO; 89 (LO RT), Raul Touzon/NGIC; 90-91 (BACK), Roman Sigaev/SS; 90 (UP), Gary Crabbe/AL; 90 (LO), Danita Delimont/AL; 91 (UP), Ben Cooper/Science Faction/GI; 91 (CTR), Taylor S. Kennedy/NGIC; 91 (LO), Gavin Hellier/Robert Harding/GI; 92 (UP), Michael DeYoung/Alaska Stock LLC/CO; 92 (LO), Patrick Endres/Alaska Stock LLC/CO; 93 (UP), Bill Hutchinson/NGIC; 93 (CTR), Galen Rowell/Mountain Light/AL; 93 (LO LE), Accent Alaska/AL; 93 (LO RT), Kennan Ward/CO; 94-95 (BACK), Roman Sigaev/SS; 94 (UP RT), RGB Ventures/SuperStock/AL; 94 (UP LE), AlaskaStock/CO; 94 (LO), Mark Cosslett/NGIC; 95 (UP), Tim Laman/NGIC; 95 (LO), Momatiuk - Eastcott/CO; 96 (UP), Michael Melford/NGIC; 96 (LO), Doug Marshall/Aurora Photos/CO; 97 (UP RT), Paul Chesley/NGIC; 97 (UP LE), Heath Korvola/Aurora Photos/CO; 97 (LO LE), Adam Jones/GI; 97 (LO RT), Michael Quinton/MP/NGIC; 98-99 (BACK), Roman Sigaev/SS; 98 (CTR), Doug Marshall/Aurora Photos/CO; 98 (LO LE), John Reddy; 98 (LO RT), Stephen Oachs Photography/Flickr RMGI; 99 (UP), NPS/AL; 99 (LO), Skip Brown/NGIC; 100 (UP), Eutoch/Dreamstime; 100 (CTR), Corbis Premium RF/AL; 100 (LO), James Steidl/Dreamstime; 101 (LO LE), Glenn Nagel/Dreamstime; 101 (LO CTR), Michael Elliott/Dreamstime; 101 (RT UP), Erich Schlegel/INTERNATIONAL_NI/CO; 101 (RT LO), SeaPics; 102 (UP), Tim Fitzharris/MP/NGIC; 102 (LO), Niebrugge Images/AL; 103 (UP), Gary Crabbe/Enlightened Images/AL; 103 (CTR), Paul Street/AL; 103 (LO LE), Drew Rush/NGIC; 103 (LO RT), Robbie George/NGIC; 104-105 (BACK), Roman Sigaev/SS; 104 (UP), idp grand teton collection/AL; 104 (LO), Kate Thompson/NGIC; 105 (UP), imagebroker/AL; 105 (CTR), Dan Sullivan/AL; 105 (LO), Penny De Los Santos/NGIC; 106 (UP), Guido Cozzi/CO; 106 (LO), Jens Grosser/National Geographic Your Shot/NGIC; 107 (UP), Ed Rana/National Geographic Your Shot/NGIC; 107 (CTR RT), imac/AL; 107 (LO LE), Bill Brooks/AL; 107 (LO RT), Frans Lanting/CO; 108-109 (BACK), Roman Sigaev/SS; 108 (UP), Monica and Michael Sweet/Flickr RM/GI; 108 (CTR), Maria Stenzel/NGIC; 108 (LO), Scott Darsney/Lonely Planet Images/GI; 109 (UP), Frans Lanting/CO; 109 (LO), MacDuff Everton/NGIC; 110 (UP), Frans Lanting/NGIC; 110 (LO), Charles Gipstein/NGIC; 111 (UP), Tom Pfeiffer/Flickr RM/GI; 111 (CTR), Steve and Donna O'Meara/NGIC; 111 (LO LE), Danita Delimont/AL; 111 (LO RT), Darlyne Murawski/NGIC; 112-103 (BACK), Roman Sigaev/SS; 112 (UP LE), Jerry Driendl/The Image Bank/GI; 112 (UP RT), Dave Jepson/AL; 112 (LO), Matthew Botos/AL; 113 (UP), Photo Resource Hawaii/AL; 113 (LO), nagelestock/AL; 114 (UP), Tim Fitzharris/MP/NGIC; 114 (LO), Michael and Patricia Fogden/MP/NGIC; 115 (UP), Richard Broadwell/AL; 115 (CTR), NGIC/AL; 115 (LO LE), Don Mason/Blend Images LLC/CO; 115 (LO RT), Jack Goldfarb/Design Pics/CO; 116-117 (BACK), Roman Sigaev/SS; 116 (UP LE), Tim Laman/NGIC; 116 (UP RT), Rick Edwards ARPS/AL; 116 (LO LE), David Davis/SS; 116 (LO RT), Tom Sebourn/SS; 117 (UP), Ben Horton/NGIC; 118 (UP), Tim Fitzharris/MP/NGIC; 118 (LO), Alexis Valentin/National Geographic Your Shot/NGIC; 119 (UP RT), courtesy Crystal Mountain Resort, Jason Anglin; 119 (UP LE), imagebroker/AL; 119 (LO LE), Stephen Matera/Aurora Photos/CO; 119 (LO RT), Konrad Wothe/MP/NGIC; 120-121 (BACK), Roman Sigaev/SS; 120 (UP), Brad Mitchell Bradley/AL; 120 (LO), Ivan Stanic/SS; 121 (UP), Zach Holmes/AL; 121 (CTR), neelsky/SS; 121 (LO), Image Source/CO; 122 (UP), Keneva Photography/SS; 122 (CTR), Dan Leeth/AL; 122 (LO), WaterFrame/AL; 123 (UP), Juan Carlos Munoz/Adobe Stock Photo; 123 (CTR RT), Witold Skrypczak/AL; 123 (LO LE), Jim West/AL; 124 (UP), Stuart Westmorland/CO; 124 (LO), Pat O'Hara/CO; 125 (UP), Ocean/CO; 125 (CTR), Chris Cheadle/CO; 125 (LO LE), Rob Casey/GI; 125 (LO RT), Tom Reichner/SS; 126-127 (BACK), Roman Sigaev/SS; 126 (UP), Tim Laman/NGIC; 126 (LO LE), Konrad Wothe/MP/NGIC; 126 (LO RT), Nick Hall/CO; 127 (UP), Don Curry/National Geographic Your Shot/NGIC; 127 (LO), Jami Garrison/SS; 128 (UP), Justin Calkins/National Geographic Your Shot/NGIC; 128 (LO), Paul Chesley/NGIC; 129 (UP RT), Richard T. Nowitz/CO; 129 (UP LE), Tim Fitzharris/MP/NGIC; 129 (LO LE), Richard Nowitz/NGIC; 129 (LO RT), Richard Hahn/National Geographic Your Shot/NGIC; 130-131 (BACK), Roman Sigaev/SS; 130 (UP), Sergio Ballivian/Aurora Open/CO; 130 (CTR), Sasha Buzko/SS; 130 (LO), Stock Connection Distribution/AL; 131 (CTR), Richard Nowitz/NGIC; 131 (LO), Richard Nowitz/NGIC; 132 (UP), Paul Souders/CO; 132 (LO), Michael Melford/NGIC; 133 (UP LE), Annie Griffiths Belt/CO; 133 (UP RT), PhotoXite/SS; 133 (LO LE), TMI/AL; 133 (LO RT), Ocean/CO; 134-135 (BACK), Roman Sigaev/SS; 134 (UP), Frans Lanting/NGIC; 134 (LO), Norbert Rosing/NGIC; 135 (UP), Fotofeeling/Westend61/CO; 135 (CTR), Drew Rush/NGIC; 135 (LO), Amar and Isabelle Guillen - Guillen Photography/AL; 136 (UP), Katrina Leigh/SS; 136 (LO), Lake County Museum/CO; 137 (UP), Heath Korvola/GI; 137 (CTR), John & Lisa Merrill/GI; 137 (LO LE), Michael Melford/NGIC; 137 (LO RT), Tom Brakefield/Brand X/GI; 138-139 (BACK), Roman Sigaev/SS; 138 (UP), Harry Thomas/iStockphoto; 138 (LO), Rough Guides/Paul Whitfield/GI; 139 (UP), Bill Hatcher/NGIC; 139 (CTR), pmphoto/SS; 139 (LO), Dean Conger/NGIC; 140 (UP), Momatiuk - Eastcott/CO; 140 (LO), Ruaridh Stewart/Zuma Press/CO; 141 (UP RT), Kirk Mastin/Aurora Photos/CO; 141 (UP LE), Danita Delimont/Gallo Images/GI; 141 (LO LE), Craig Ruaux/AL; 141 (LO RT), Alan Copson/JAI/CO; 142-143 (BACK), Roman Sigaev/SS; 142 (UP), Jim Parkin/AL; 142 (LO), Dennis MacDonald/AL; 143 (UP), Tetra Images/AL; 143 (CTR), IMAGEMORE Co., Ltd./AL; 143 (LO), Russ Bishop/AL; 144 (UP LE), John Warburton-Lee/JAI/CO; 144 (UP RT), Danita Delimont/GI; 144 (LO), Sumikophoto/Dreamstime; 145 (UP LE), Ed Freeman/GI; 145 (CTR RT), Citizen of the Planet/AL; 145 (LO), Pat Canova/AL; 146, John Eascott and Yva Momatuik/NGIC; 149, Bryan Peterson/The Image Bank/GI; **MORE NATIONAL PARKS:** 150-151, Randy Olson/NGIC; 152 (UP), Supri Suharjoto/SS; 152 (LO), Matthijs Wetterauw/SS; 153 (UP), Dick Durrance II/NGIC; 153 (LO), mlorenz/SS; 154 (UP LE), Shane W Thompson/SS; 154 (UP RT), Cathleen A Clapper/SS; 154 (LO), Mark Musselman/NGIC; 155 (UP), gary yim/SS; 155 (LO LE), Sylvie Bouchard/SS; 155 (LO RT), 4cornersphoto/SS; 156 (UP LE), Cosmin Manci/SS; 156 (UP RT), MountainHardcore/SS; 157 (UP), Maxim Kulko/SS; 157 (LO), Steve Estvanik/SS; 158 (UP), David Maska/SS; 158 (LO), Jagodka/SS; 159, SS; 160 (UP), fivespots/SS; 160 (LO), jadimages/SS; 161 (CTR), Rich Carey/SS; 161 (UP), N. Frey Photography/SS; 161 (LO), Vereshchagin Dmitry/SS

National Geographic gratefully acknowledges the National Park Trust for use of its mascot, Buddy Bison.

STAFF FOR THIS BOOK
Priyanka Lamichhane, *Project Editor*
James Hiscott, Jr., *Art Director*
Lori Epstein, *Senior Illustrations Editor*
Allison O'Brien Muff, *Photo Editor*
Dawn McFadden, *Designer*
Debbie Gibbons, *Director of Intracompany Cartography*
Matt W. Chwastyk, Michael McNey, Gregory Ugiansky, Martin S. Walz, *Map Research and Production*
Grace Hill, *Managing Editor*
Joan Gossett, Alix Inchausti, *Production Editors*
Lewis R. Bassford, *Production Manager*
Darrick McRae, *Manager, Production Services*
Susan Borke, *Legal and Business Affairs*
Kate Olesin, Angela Modany, *Assistant Editors*
Kathryn Robbins, Sanjida Rashid, Rachel Kenny, *Design Production Assistants*
Hillary Moloney, *Illustrations Assistant*

SENIOR MANAGEMENT TEAM, KIDS PUBLISHING AND MEDIA
Nancy Laties Feresten, *Senior Vice President*; Erica Green, *Vice President, Editorial Director, Kids Books*; Julie Vosburgh Agnone, *Vice President, Operations*; Jennifer Emmett, *Vice President, Content*; Michelle Sullivan, *Vice President, Video and Digital Initiatives*; Eva Absher-Schantz, *Vice President, Visual Identity*; Rachel Buchholz, *Editor and Vice President, NG Kids magazine*; Jay Sumner, *Photo Director*; Amanda Larsen, *Design Director, Kids Books*; Hannah August, *Marketing Director*; R. Gary Colbert, *Production Director*

DIGITAL
Laura Goertzel, *Manager*; Sara Zeglin, *Senior Producer*; Bianca Bowman, *Assistant Producer*; Natalie Jones, *Senior Product Manager*

Published by National Geographic Partners, LLC

Copyright © 2012, 2016 National Geographic Society. All rights reserved. Reproduction of the whole or any part of the contents without written permission from the publisher is prohibited.

NATIONAL GEOGRAPHIC and Yellow Border Design are trademarks of the National Geographic Society, used under license.

Since 1888, the National Geographic Society has funded more than 14,000 research, conservation, education, and storytelling projects around the world. National Geographic Partners distributes a portion of the funds it receives from your purchase to National Geographic Society to support programs including the conservation of animals and their habitats. To learn more, visit natgeo.com/info.

For more information, visit nationalgeographic.com, call 1-877-873-6846, or write to the following address:

National Geographic Partners, LLC
1145 17th Street NW
Washington, DC 20036-4688 U.S.A.

More for kids from National Geographic: natgeokids.com

National Geographic Kids magazine inspires children to explore their world with fun yet educational articles on animals, science, nature, and more. Using fresh storytelling and amazing photography, *Nat Geo Kids* shows kids ages 6 to 14 the fascinating truth about the world—and why they should care. natgeo.com/subscribe

For rights or permissions inquiries, please contact National Geographic Books Subsidiary Rights: bookrights@natgeo.com

The Library of Congress cataloged the 2012 edition as follows:
National Geographic kids national parks guide U.S.A. : the most amazing sights, scenes, and cool activities from coast to coast / National Geographic.
    p. cm.
Includes index.
ISBN 978-1-4263-0932-8 (library binding : alk. paper) — ISBN 978-1-4263-0931-1 (pbk. : alk. paper)
1. National parks and reserves—United States—Guidebooks—Juvenile literature. 2. United States—Description and travel—Guidebooks—Juvenile literature. I. National Geographic Society (U.S.)
E160.N2434 2012
917.3'04—dc23
                        2011034235

2016 trade paperback ISBN: 978-1-4263-2314-0
2016 reinforced library binding ISBN: 978-1-4263-2315-7

Neither the publisher nor the author shall be liable for any bodily harm that may be caused or sustained as a result of conducting any of the activities described in this book.

The web addresses and other information presented in this book were current as of the initial publication date.

Buddy Bison appears 27 times throughout this book.

For more information about our National Parks, visit natgeo.com/kids/parks.

Printed in the United States of America
24/VP/9

176